Vanessa G

MW01093292

SURVIVING CHANGE AT WORK

MORE FROM A BOOK APART

You Deserve a Tech Union
Ethan Marcotte

Design by Definition
Elizabeth McGuane

Wireframing for Everyone
Michael Angeles, Leon Barnard, and Billy Carlson

Immersive Content and Usability
Preston So

The Business of UX Writing
Yael Ben-David

Inclusive Design Communities
Sameera Kapila

Leading Content Design
Rachel McConnell

You Should Write a Book
Katel LeDû and Lisa Maria Marquis

Responsible JavaScript
Jeremy Wagner

SEO for Everyone
Rebekah Baggs and Chris Corak

Visit abookapart.com for our full list of titles.

Copyright © 2023 Vanessa Gennarelli
All rights reserved

Publisher: Jeffrey Zeldman
Designer: Jason Santa Maria
Executive director: Katel LeDû
Editor in chief: Lisa Maria Marquis
Editors: Jen Mediano, Caren Litherland
Book producer: Ron Bilodeau

ISBN: 978-1-952616-62-4

A Book Apart
New York, New York
http://abookapart.com

10 9 8 7 6 5 4 3 2 1

TABLE OF CONTENTS

Thanks, Mom

FOREWORD

Change is a stranger you have yet to know.
—GEORGE MICHAEL

IN OUR MODERN, technology-driven lives, one thing has become abundantly clear: change shapes our existence. The COVID-19 pandemic, in particular, served as a stark reminder of just how rapidly and profoundly our world can transform. It forced us to adapt, to reimagine the way we work, and to confront the inevitability of change head-on. The question, "Where do you see yourself in five years?" suddenly didn't have a clear answer.

I first met Vanessa when she was leading things over at GitHub Education, and reconnected with her recently, after she and I had both gone through many job changes and large organizational shifts. Through the years, we've hit bumps along the path as our companies experienced acquisitions, and growth, and layoffs (oh my!).

I've been at small and large startups, and experienced the ups and downs of finding market fit and creating a growth trajectory. I've worked with companies struggling to survive, and with leaders who weren't sure how to handle their company's success. While these changes are normal and even common, effective guidance and wisdom around navigating them as an employee is hard to come by. We shouldn't have to guess our way through "figuring it out" in order to overcome uncertainty when a big shift comes our way at work!

This is the handbook I wish I'd had in the moments I didn't know what to expect. Vanessa doesn't hold back, sharing practical, firsthand advice for cultivating the mindset necessary to make change work for your career. If you need support identifying the priorities most important to your role, getting comfortable with negotiation now that you have different responsibilities, or keeping up with the changes happening around you at work, this book is for you.

As you read these pages, I hope it will become clear that *you're not alone!* Good luck, and have fun, dear reader. With the right mindset, and the tools and frameworks in this book, you can transform change from a career roadblock into an opportunity for growth.

—Cassidy Williams

INTRODUCTION

YOU JOINED YOUR CURRENT company because you love the mission, or the team, or maybe you really believe in the product. And after a few months in the role, you've settled into a groove—there's rhythm in your day-to-day routine. You have some shorthand with your colleagues, and feel a sense of confidence in your tasks. You know how the organization "works." Perhaps you're proud enough to sport the swag, or identify as a "Metamate," "Hulugan," "Intercomrade," or some such.

But one day you sense a shift—there are new approvals to wade through, or procurement becomes a thing, or there's a new VP in town with a plan to "shake things up." You squint, skeptical, perhaps annoyed. You question the need for this new red tape. Is the company changing?

Probably.

More than two thousand years ago, the Greek philosopher Heraclitus passed down some weighty wisdom about change and humanity's relationship to it:

> *No man ever steps in the same river twice, for it's not the same river and he's not the same man.*

Organizations, like rivers, are always in a state of change—expanding, contracting, evolving. If you joined an organization whose goal is light-speed growth, or the company is less than five years old, you'll find yourself at several inflection points, wondering if the company is still for you.

If this is your first (or second, or even third!) rodeo in a tech job, my book will help you through this inflection point.

The same forces that change the company as it grows, change you. They can push you to grow, to step into increasingly complex situations and roles. They can also uncover what really matters to you in your role.

Because no matter what, a change is going to come.

A big shift

I'll never forget one of the biggest shifts in my career that shaped a lot of the lessons in this book. On June 3, 2018, I woke up in South Philadelphia to my phone's insistent "buzz buzz buzz," which isn't unusual for a tech job. The longer you work in this industry, the more likely it is that companies entrust you with responsibility. "Responsibility" often means more notifications.

At the time, I led the education team at GitHub, which served over a million students across a portfolio of products and programs. If you've supported a product before, then you're well aware of the sheer volume of inbound requests, alerts, and incidents that pose time-sensitive bids for attention. Most of my mornings began with a triage that started as soon as I woke up.

When I clumsily clawed my hand around my phone to read that morning's alerts, I could barely parse the words lit up on the screen. *The Verge* reported: "Microsoft has reportedly acquired GitHub—deal could be announced on Monday."

I was already overwhelmed. Between offsite meetings, conferences, workshops and the like, I was on the road more than a hundred days a year. My emotional capacity to handle surprises—of any size—was zero. As I continued to read, my frame of mind darted from confusion to fear to frustration.

Was this good news? Every startup wants a profitable exit. Was it bad news? Our team of six could easily be made redundant by our *many* counterparts across the expansive terrain of Microsoft's Redmond campus. Was I out of a job? Was this a hostile takeover? What would I tell my team?

As I struggled to make sense of the headlines, field the many frenetic notifications, and sort out my own feelings about the rigamarole, I felt alone. No one could answer my questions. No one could set expectations. The information vacuum quickly bred suspicion.

I found myself in the middle of a big shift, and I quickly learned one of the first lessons of this book: while it can feel as though these changes are happening *to you,* you have more agency than you realize.

You can roll with change by diagnosing the situation, working through likely scenarios, weighing where the organization might invest their resources, and using time-tested patterns to anticipate the company's next steps.

How to use this book

From the experience of supporting my team through Microsoft's acquisition, along with my previous roles in rapidly growing companies, I learned how to navigate uncertainty, and detect patterns about how companies behave. What follows is a massive shortcut: the stories, exercises, and scholarly research I've boiled down to a trim hundred pages or so represent more than fifteen years of experience across seven tech organizations, four years of leadership coaching, and graduate degrees from Harvard (Education) and Stanford (Business).

This is a handbook to help you survive and thrive in the face of change. It brings together essential knowledge from several areas:

- **Business and Company Life Cycle 101.** Understanding a company's stage of development and next steps makes for more informed decision-making.
- **Strategies for planning your career.** We'll use tools to help you identify your priorities, weigh what's important to you, and develop a strategy to grow into your next role.
- **Persuasion and influence.** Knowing what you want is half the battle—the other half requires framing your ideas in ways that appeal to your manager, VP, or CEO.
- **Navigating shifts in your company's culture.** We'll dig into how the culture will transform as it matures—and how to navigate the evolving systems and structures.
- **Leading through change.** I'll introduce you to a lightweight framework to motivate and sustain changes to processes, expectations, and team structure.
- **Moving on.** We'll create a blueprint for leaving an organization on good terms when it's time for you to transition to your next chapter.

This book brings together highlights and original research from CEOs, managers, and individual contributors at rapidly growing companies—like SendGrid, MongoDB, Twilio, and Stripe—who have lived to tell the tale. By the time you reach the end, you'll have a roadmap for your future. You'll be able to anticipate your organization's next steps, possess strategies to sell your ideas internally, and know how to lead through change successfully.

Why this book is for you

If you've been dreading change, you're not alone—we'll start there.

If you want to make the chaos of a tech job work for you and get the most out of the opportunities that come out of change, this book is for you.

If you're emotionally connected to your company and you're scared that significant change will fundamentally alter what you like about your current gig, this book will save you hours, weeks, and potentially months of strife and heartache.

Let's begin.

1

THE THIRTY-THOUSAND-FOOT VIEW

FOR THOSE OF US PRIVILEGED enough to work in the tech sector, we know it's not always hearts and rainbows about "impacting the future." Some days can be challenging, sure. But if meetings begin to feel like a ten-round boxing match, or your boss isn't hearing you, or you find yourself complaining about work to your friends and family, these are signals. Work doesn't have to be so *hard*.

It's time to take a step back and look at the bigger picture: Where is your company *going*? From a thirty-thousand-foot vantage point, are you and the company swimming in the same direction, or at cross-purposes? Understanding a company's demands, pressures, and goals can help us get perspective.

KNOW YOUR LIFE CYCLE

The notion of a *life cycle* breaks up stages of development into phases, helping us understand a dynamic process in a deeper way. Science uses this concept to explain mitosis or the quarters of the moon, or the lifecycle of a star for example. When we view a life cycle as a series of phases, we get a sense of what is unique to each stage, and gain insight into *what happens next*.

Understanding a company's life cycle is a "cheat mode": you can see into the future and prepare for the shifts that are probably coming your way. Each phase presents new challenges for the organization, and, for you as an employee, specific risks and opportunities. Once you have a sense of where a company is in its life cycle, the ups and downs of pivoting, scaling, and maturing are easier to navigate.

PHASES OF A RAPID-GROWTH ORGANIZATION

Products, processes, and companies break at consistent inflection points. My former manager, Shanku Niyogi, now the Chief Product Officer at Databricks, would remind me how this pattern applies to product development:

> *You build your first iteration of the product to go from 1 to 10, then you have to rewrite to scale from 10 to 100, and then to 1,000.*

At each phase of a codebase rewrite, the team building the product needs to reassess the short- and long-term business goals, feedback from customers, and market trends. As the product matures, each rewrite brings the opportunity for change—and for you to make an impact.

The same pattern applies to organizations. When counseling his students about their careers, entrepreneur and marketing professor Scott Galloway compares the life cycle of businesses to the alphabet:

> *Think of companies and products having a life cycle, A-Z. Are you happiest at start-ups where you're expected to wear a number of different hats (A-D), the inception/visionary stage (E-H), good at managing, scaling, and reinventing (I-P)... or can you manage a firm/product in decline, and do so profitably*

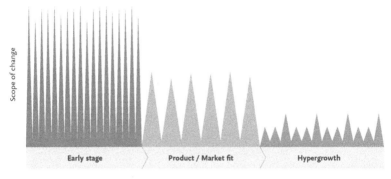

FIG 1.1: This diagram shows the life cycle of a rapidly growing organization and how employees experience change: in the early stage, change is constant and wide-ranging, and as the company matures, change is smaller, but still frequent.

(Q-Z)? Few people are good across more than several letters. This exercise should help guide the firms and projects you work for and pursue. (https://bkaprt.com/scw48/01-01)

Since many of the companies we work for may not even see the end of the alphabet, let's simplify Galloway's formula to three life cycle stages: *early, product / market fit,* and *hypergrowth* (FIG 1.1). During each phase, organizations prioritize different areas of the business, their culture gets stress-tested by different questions, and the expectations for efficiency change over time.

Let's dig into each phase in more detail. Once you recognize where your company lands in the life cycle, you'll have a better sense of what comes next.

Early phase

In an early-stage organization, you're running on vision, serotonin, and midnight oil. The rapid-fire rate of change, shoestring budgets, and ambiguous goals are not for the faint of heart.

Core attributes

Your customer and target market may not be clear at this stage. Research and development—engineering and product activities—take up all of the focus. Expectations around product and code quality lie somewhere around "good enough." Human resources is often just a tool set: a payroll provider and some compliance paperwork. You know you're in an early-phase organization if:

- It's almost entirely focused on research and development.
- Hiring is exclusive to engineering and product.
- Roles tend to be larger and more ambiguous.
- The decision-making process is ad hoc and/or intuitive.
- Everything is temporary: change is dramatic, drastic, and constant.

Risks

It's worth underscoring that early-stage companies are the riskiest to join, made even riskier if the company has accepted venture capital. Venture capital demands a big return, and that additional pressure forces organizations to follow scalable ideas. Here are a few risks to be aware of:

- The organization may suddenly change direction—this may mean your skills are no longer a fit.
- The company may not become financially solvent, which could leave you looking for a job.
- Hiring and firing cycles are part of the iteration process, so if you need job security, this isn't the stage for you.

Opportunities

The action is happening in the research and development side of the house. If that's your skill set, you can learn a lot firsthand and have autonomy to make decisions.

- Large, more ambiguous roles mean that you can make a bigger impact on the product and on the company.
- You're more likely to work directly with company founders, who are calling the shots.
- You can negotiate for a bigger or more impressive job title, since many early-stage organizations can't offer other benefits.

Product / market-fit phase

The first sign that your company is in this phase might be the influx of new team members, so many that you don't know all of them by name. You'll definitely notice when your company has more than 150 employees, which is thought to be the maximum number of relationships one human can reasonably maintain, called *Dunbar's number* after British anthropologist Robin Dunbar (https://bkaprt.com/scw48/01-02). When a company hits that number of employees, you begin to encounter both technical and cultural debt; systems can't scale past their current configuration without being revamped. Dana Lawson, senior vice president of engineering at Netlify, told me how decision-making can slow down with the infusion of new people:

> When you're around Dunbar's number, that's when you can't walk down the hallway to talk to the person to get things done. You can't make decisions quickly. People become more transactional, because they don't know each other personally. As your portfolio grows, the number of products and features you have to support goes way up.

At this stage, top-level goals change frequently, and you can feel a fair amount of whiplash. Lynn Wallenstein, senior vice president of engineering at CargoSense, told me it's helpful to think of this phase as a sort of adolescence:

> The organization is figuring itself out. It's a teenager. A teenager tries on personalities, figuring out who they want to be. The company will behave that way for a certain period of

time. That's very hard if you hold on to expectations or goals too tightly.

At the same time, the pressure to grow will translate to investment in sales and marketing. Rick Nucci, CEO of Guru, told me he frames the early stage as "0 to 1" (with product / market fit as "1 to 10" and Hypergrowth as "10 to 100"), and clearly calls out which stage the company is in when he holds town halls and all-hands meetings:

> *If I'm talking to a salesperson at Guru, at 0 to 1, you're trying to get those first people excited about your product and pay money for it. Repeatability doesn't matter yet. It's "Will anyone actually pay money for this product?" At 1 to 10 we're focusing on a repeatable way to acquire customers, and figuring out if can we do it in a way that's scalable. These are two different things.*

Core attributes

As the organization reaches product / market fit, a bit of process begins to firm up. You know the customer you serve, and you're earning some money through early customers or self-serve motions. Departments get formalized, managers with deep domain expertise are hired to lead them, and specialized skill sets become the norm. Here are a few of the patterns you'll see at this stage:

- Early general and administrative hires come on board, especially in finance.
- The organization gains some structure: functions and departments form with expert leadership.
- Smaller "subcommunities" take shape within the company at the department or team level.
- Market demands and customer behavior inform the decision-making process, making it more data-driven.
- Your customers aren't just pulling out a credit card; they're engaging in longer-term arrangements. You'll need to meet their expectations around security and regulatory compliance.

Risks

During this phase, the company will continue to change its mind about direction and goals. You may not have high-level goals; or, if you do, they change on a dime. Here are some of the risks associated with these 180-degree shifts:

- The organization has few procedures to lean on when things go wrong. Yes, there should probably be a process or documentation, but it hasn't been a priority among all the other pressing demands on people's time.
- It's hard to consistently forecast sales or allocate funding, so any change in demand can overwhelm support, cause down time in your product, or lead to delays in service.
- The company may be growing faster than it can reasonably hire and train people.
- Employees who were part of the early-stage "old guard" move on—because they prefer early-stage companies, or because the company needs leaders who have more experience. The disappointment can be hard, and leadership transitions are rocky. More on that later.

Opportunities

Organizations that have found product / market fit are safer bets to join than early-stage organizations. One big opportunity in this phase is experimenting with customer acquisition strategies. This piece is crucial for the organization to get right for the profitability and health of the company. It shouldn't invest heavily in any one growth mechanism that doesn't make sense over the long haul. Other opportunities include:

- As an early employee, you can get a bigger chunk of equity.
- You might choose to step up and try a larger role when someone moves on.
- Clearly articulated levels, salary bands, and other human-resources systems are unlikely to exist at this stage. Negotiate.

Hypergrowth phase

Once the mission-critical pieces of the business are in place—your company has demonstrated demand for your product, it's replicable, and it has grabbed a chunk of market share—you've reached the hypergrowth phase.

Hypergrowth, which I'll use interchangeably with *scale*, means it's time to serve more customers, or more geographic regions, or perhaps even to expand to operate in new verticals. And it *hurts*.

At this point, the organization is tracking toward an "exit," also known as a "liquidity event," like an acquisition or an initial public offering (IPO). The organization will need to get its fiduciary house in order to unlock maximum coin. Even research and development (R & D) will have to measure expenditures and keep spending in check for a good contribution margin.

You'll notice more formalized departments headed up by leaders who own decision-making abilities in their area. Rick Nucci told me that he consciously takes this step as his companies reach hypergrowth:

> *[This stage] is when you have to intentionally shift leadership responsibilities. It's where you build out a leadership team. As the CEO, I remove myself from a lot of the decision-making in favor of giving others autonomy and empowerment.*

Core attributes

At this level, your customers depend on you and expect a high level of quality. They won't accept outages, slow performance, or inefficiency. Other consistent signs you're in the hypergrowth phase include the following:

· Expectations for user growth skyrocket.
· CEOs may raise additional funding to support growth, and direct those funds to sales, marketing, customer success, and services departments.

- You'll notice that more folks join the company with "operations" in their titles (sales ops, business ops, product ops, marketing ops) to help the business scale.
- Decision-making shifts from founders to department heads, who likely have more expertise in their particular domain.
- You might see top-level goals and direction for the first time, such as key performance indicators (KPIs) to proactively plan initiatives and measure success.
- Slower, more structured change touches every area of the organization as it matures.

Risks

Toward the end of this phase, you'll begin to detach from the momentum of the original vision, that "change-the-world" energy or early puppylike creativity. If you've been with the organization since its early days, the additional layers of operations and compliance can make you feel like you're moving through mud. A few general signs of hypergrowth that many folks struggle with are:

- Your autonomy and latitude to make decisions may feel stifled. There are processes in place to convince gatekeepers, who exist to maintain quality.
- Mission drift happens when market demands take precedence.
- You'll find you have less direct access to the founders, or to the new leadership team. Leadership can feel disconnected from the rank and file—an "us versus them" narrative can take hold.
- The culture changes from an R & D-driven focus to a sales-driven orientation. The organization puts a lot of focus on sales, since so many of its performance goals center on revenue and user growth.
- The organization will trim the excesses of the early days—think fewer fringe benefits, fancy offices, or cushy budgets for the latest gear. Financial fitness becomes chiefly important. Leadership may consider layoffs in order to appeal to an acquirer, or to prepare for an IPO.

Opportunities

One huge opportunity here is to learn from domain experts and leadership. You'll see more leaders in the company, with additional managers and directors supporting them. That will likely translate to you having a new boss, which we'll dig into later.

- Hopefully, by now, experts in roles can offer mentorship to earlier-in-career folks.
- Roles and expectations become clearly defined, with levels and performance reviews. You'll know what is expected of you.
- Everyone's still motivated to get things done. Now's the time to meet, work with, and grow your network.

Your analysis

As you read through the various life-cycle phases, did you spot any traits or problems that you encounter in your day-to-day work? As you think about the challenges facing your company, ask yourself the following questions:

- Where in the life cycle is my company currently?
- Which challenges will the company soon face?
- Which areas will the company prioritize and invest in?
- How might I use those changes to my advantage?
- In which phase am I most comfortable? (If you've had a few previous roles, perhaps reflect on the size and maturity of those companies.)
- What's my tolerance for risk? For change?

Understanding the life cycle imbues you with three powerful advantages: the ability to anticipate next steps, predict where resources might flow, and decide if you wish to take the next step with your current company.

If your company is technology-focused and has its sights set on growth, it will feel these challenges. Understanding them, and then digesting what that means for your everyday work, will set you up for success.

Graham Neray, CEO of Oso and former chief of staff at MongoDB, has seen how shifting one's perspective from "my work" to "the company's next priorities" has made whole careers. Neray joined MongoDB as a product marketing manager in 2012. As the organization grew from product / market fit to hypergrowth, his role changed four times. He was able to ride the chaos that an early-stage company goes through and makes those changes work *for* him.

To hear Graham tell it, that kind of alignment and awareness is rocket fuel for one's career:

> *I've seen a switch flip, where suddenly someone understands how to make their personal career goals mesh with where the organization is going. Rapidly growing companies want to promote from within, and if you have an ownership mindset where you understand the trade-offs and the higher-level goals, that makes a huge difference on your trajectory inside the company. And those people, at least at MongoDB, got promoted faster, got more responsibility, got more respect from higher leadership, because they weren't necessarily optimizing for themselves or for their team, but contextualizing where their team goals fit into the broader company goals.*

Where the organization is going, *broader company goals*, *tradeoffs*—all are key signals that will tell you what's next.

An organization's goals drive where the money goes

Each phase of an organization's life cycle is stress-tested to meet different goals: *Can we make a product, is it commercially viable*, and *can it scale profitably*? To meet those goals, leaders make bets in the form of investments.

As you may have guessed by now, those bets will change as the organization matures. Now that you have a sense of where in the life cycle your own company is, you can reasonably project the sorts of goals it's tracking toward now, and what those goals might look like in the near future.

To start, think of the organization's budget as a pie. During the early stage, that pie might be evenly split between product and engineering (a.k.a. research and development, or R & D), with a small sliver of operations. The product / market-fit phase will dedicate a larger slice to marketing and finance. Hyper-growth will need to boost sales and operational efficiency, so the pie will split across those lines.

Since money is a scarce and finite resource, your company's leaders will make their bets strategically.

Strategy: Where would you invest?

Let's make you the CEO of your company for a moment. When you analyze the company at a high level, with all the challenges you're facing, where would you invest? The goal of this exercise is to connect strategy with a corresponding investment.

We'll start with a use case that's dear to my heart: the world of HGTV. Say you need to renovate your home to sell it for the highest price, and you have $100 to spend on the renovation. The realtors tell you that buyers decide based on curb appeal, kitchens, and bathrooms. Your strategy might be to spend $50 in the kitchen, $30 on the bathroom, and the remaining $20 on the exterior.

Now, say you had a budget of $100 to invest in the organization—this is the pie you'll be working with. You know from the life-cycle data which challenges the organization will need to overcome, and the goals it will likely set as a result.

- *Where* would you invest it? (Which department? Which initiative?)
- *What results* would you expect to see (in terms of cost reduction, growth, revenue, etc.)?

For example, if an organization is trying to go public, they might spend $30 on boosting efficiency and operations, $40 on sales, and $30 on engineering to develop features to compete in the market. The results they would expect to see, respectively, are a good margin, increased pipeline value, and a boost in sales. Or, put another way:

DEPARTMENT	INITIATIVE	BUDGET	EXPECTED RESULT
Finance	Budgeting and tracking	$30	Boost gross profit margin
Sales	Regional expansion	$40	Increase value of pipeline
Engineering	Packaging and pricing	$30	Boost sales against competition

While it's a simple sketch, this framing is basically what leaders do on the regular: they make investments that they believe will drive toward goals. It's a hypothesis for sure, as is your sketch here. There are a lot of ways to add up to a hundred, though most organizations focus on a few priorities at a time.

Speaking of priorities, when framing your expected return on investment (ROI)—for any initiative, as well as for your own role—you're driving toward one of two themes:

- Increasing something—user base, revenue, gross margin, pipeline
- Decreasing something—cost, time, number of roles allocated

Here are a few examples of top-level goals from departments across a company. This will give you a sample of the levers they might pull in order to achieve the ROI, the end result:

- A sales department implements a customer success team to increase activation.
- A marketing team launches an email campaign to increase user acquisition.

- A product team changes the onboarding process to reduce churn.
- A finance department cuts travel and entertainment to increase margin.
- A legal team automates the ten most common contract forms to reduce days to deal closed.
- A human resources department increases equity offer to increase the percentage of candidate acceptance.
- An operations team invests in quality assurance to decrease defects per ten thousand units.
- A support team creates a self-serve portal to increase the response rate of inbound requests in twenty-four hours.

Now that you can see the company's decisions and priorities in terms of *investments*, let's take a look at how your role contributes to the big picture.

WHAT'S YOUR ROI?

Seen at the thirty-thousand-foot view, is your role within the company...

- an investment the company makes to meet its goals, or
- a unique blend of your talent, education, and expertise?

So many of us equate our jobs with our value as people, and when that value is questioned, we take it personally. But once we see our roles as investments, not only does it become easier to see how we contribute to the big picture, but it also puts us in a more confident place to negotiate with the company. You know how you contribute, and it's a specific dollar amount.

This can feel awkward, especially for individuals who value intangibles like relationships or quality work. Keep repeating your ROI in meetings, to new colleagues, to people who ask what you do at dinner parties. The more you say your ROI out loud, the less reactive or scary it feels to prove your worth.

If you haven't thought about your role in this way before, let's look at a few thought exercises to help you find your ROI.

ROI calculator

Your ROI is the value your role creates in exchange for your salary. To get a well-rounded picture of your ROI, think about it in terms of who you serve. Think about how do you generate value for:

- External users (or clients) of your product or service, whether they are businesses (B2B), or individuals (B2C).
- Internal teams at your company, particularly if you work in a centralized team, as within a service organization.
- Your direct team, through leadership or support.
- The organization that employs you as a whole.

Having this information ready to reference goes a long way toward getting more resources, making the case for promotion, and increasing the longer-term security of your role (FIG 1.2-3).

Take this practical example: GitHub Education worked with students, who would integrate Git and GitHub into their workflows early in their careers. The team blossomed from four scrappy team members to a twenty-four-person-strong organization with product, engineering, marketing, and partnership functions. Why? Because we could draw a line directly from each dollar we spent to the eventual lifetime value of a customer. Students were some of the most active users on the platform, which also ticked the "engagement" box. When your ROI is tight, the work sells itself.

Building a track record

Projects that can't tie their work directly to a return on investment have less security over the long term. Budgets that seem "bubbly," outsized, or lavish will get cut as the organization matures. If your ROI is good vibes, you're vulnerable.

Projects that can draw a straight line from their activities to money will have more staying power. If your team contributes to the core offering or to the product that's a competitive advantage against the competition, you'll get (and keep) investment.

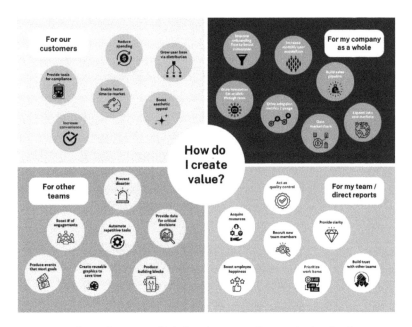

FIG 1.2: To understand your ROI, think about how your efforts resolve in value for: external customers, internal colleagues, the business broadly, and for your direct team.

WHAT'S THE ROI FOR MY ROLE?	WHAT'S THE ROI FOR MY TEAM?	WHAT'S THE ROI FOR MY PRODUCT?
Example: I bring in 6,000 accounts a year, with each account worth $10,000	*Example: My team sends 1M emails a year with a conversion rate of 1.8%. Those conversions turn into 1.2M of revenue.*	*Example: Our product in the healthcare toolchain saves technicians 14 days a year, or $5 million.*

FIG 1.3: This is an example of the ROI an account manager might calculate while working on a healthcare monitoring product.

Capitalize on the opportunity as the business matures; you can stand apart as the owner of a tremendously successful initiative, with receipts. Tracking your output helps make your case for promotion, shapes your resume, and provides a convincing argument for additional investment for your projects.

ADAPTING TO THE NEXT PHASE

Sometimes you can't stop things from happening, and being able to recognize that is a strategic skill. I've seen so many people thrash against that reality, including myself.

During Microsoft's acquisition of GitHub, it took me longer than a hot second to realize that Microsoft was a big, strong organization that would deeply influence GitHub's future.

When you look at your sketch of what's next for the company, you have a choice: to accept the organization as it is or to take a step back from it and follow another path. That choice is yours alone. You're 100 percent in control of it. Rick Nucci told me that he encourages employees to have these conversations with themselves in order to foster that self-awareness:

When the company has moved from one phase to another, it's really an intentional behavior switch. The company goes through these clearly articulated inflection points. Then, the employee can react to them in one of two ways: "This feels different—I don't feel like I'm being successful." Maybe they realize the [early stage] is what gives them energy. We've had people leave Guru for this very healthy reason, which is great. It's a self-awareness thing. They really understand what they want.

The common denominator of people who thrive across all three phases is not just a willingness to adapt, but a desire to adapt. I'm using the word "adapt" intentionally. The person says to themselves, "I see what's happening. I see that there are different chapters. And what we were doing before has to be different now. Cool. I want to do that."

Once we accept and integrate the facts about a company's next steps, new opportunities open up, like light peeking through the cracks. For my role at GitHub, being part of a larger, more mature company allowed me to grow, touch more lives, and have a bigger impact. That's a trade-off I was willing to make when I took a step forward with the organization.

I refer to this process as *finding alignment.*

ALIGNMENT: RELATING TO YOUR ORGANIZATION

In your work, you're constantly relating to the organization. I think of it as an ongoing dialogue. With each new problem the organization faces, it will change to meet the challenge. The piece you're in control of is doing the internal work of discovering what you want, and pitching it in a way that harmonizes with the direction of the company. From there, the organization may change in ways that suit you, or it may go in a direction that's not for you.

When you choose to take a step forward with the company, you're accepting those changes and making an agreement (**FIG 1.4**). It's a relationship—one that's ongoing until either of you decides to pursue another path.

Shifting your mindset from a passive one—where company decisions happen to you—to an active one—where you bring about change through your own energy and momentum—doesn't happen overnight. Diana Chapman of the Conscious Leadership Group has done some magnificent work in this area if you'd like to pursue it in more depth.

In the next chapter, we'll focus on your half of the relationship: discovering what you want and articulating it to the organization in a compelling way.

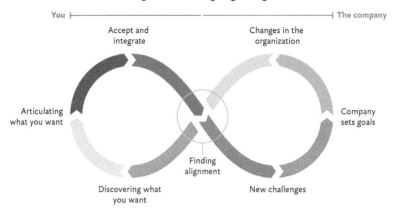

Alignment: an ongoing dialogue

You ├─────────────────────────────┤ The company

Accept and integrate

Changes in the organization

Articulating what you want

Company sets goals

Finding alignment

Discovering what you want

New challenges

FIG 1.4: Alignment is an ongoing dialogue with the company.

2

TAKE BACK THE POWER

> *What's your plan for tomorrow?*
> *Are you a leader, or will you follow?*
> *Are you a fighter, or will you cower?*
> *It's our time to take back the power.*
> —THE INTERRUPTERS

MOST OF US FEAR CHANGE, and that fear comes up in the workplace. When we look to larger companies, with wide-reaching change initiatives (pivots, reorganizations, new leadership), 70 percent of these initiatives fail, in no small part due to "employee resistance" (https://bkaprt.com/scw48/02-02). Which makes total sense: if you're in a rhythm and you like the people you work with or the projects you work on directly, any big change is a threat to your sense of control. When you begin to hear whisperings of change afoot, it can lead to thoughts of panic, scarcity, or worst-case scenarios.

But as we know, in the tech industry, change is going to come. And here's another "cheat mode" morsel: for employees at any level, big changes rip open big opportunities. If you spend time figuring out what you want, you'll be in the perfect position to jump at it during periods of change. As Philadelphia

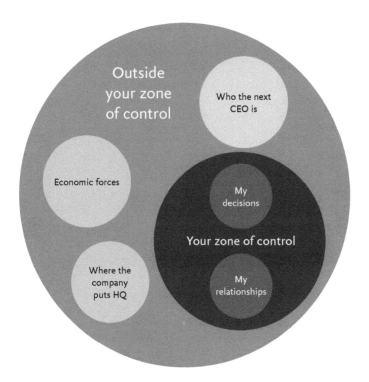

Outside your zone of control

Who the next CEO is

Economic forces

My decisions

Your zone of control

Where the company puts HQ

My relationships

FIG 2.1: Focus your energy in the areas you can control; so much of what we fret about is out of our hands entirely.

OG Benjamin Franklin said, "To succeed, jump as quickly at opportunities as you do at conclusions."

I won't claim that any role is recession-proof or change-proof, but mapping out a few options for your career can insulate you from shocks that come your way. These plans, along with your outlook, perspective, actions, and the way you see and describe your work, are all *levers that you control.*

INVEST YOUR TIME STRATEGICALLY

Focus on what's inside your *zone of control*. It's your most efficient time investment (**FIG 2.1**). You *could* spend time grinding through meeting after grueling meeting, trying to resist change or force things to go your way. But after a certain point, you're spinning your wheels resisting the inevitable. The effort and time you're putting into that resistance is a choice, however unconscious.

Tools to Take Back the Power

Here are a few ways to surface what's in your zone of control:

- *Focus* your attention on shaping your own path. The methods in this chapter will help you get clarity on the next step in your career.
- *We'll use research-backed decision-making tools* to weigh possibilities and potential outcomes.
- *Once you have a clear next step, we'll explore ways to* get proactive and start making decisions.

The journey takes a few hours, but that time investment yields swift dividends: not only will you be prepared to weather change, but you can proactively shape it.

Great leaders welcome this take-back-the-power mindset. Natalie Nagele, former CEO of Wildbit, told me that she advises employees to embrace their agency:

In our industry we have quite a bit of power—we can change jobs, try something else. Allow yourself that power. It takes a lot of anxiety away, physical stress away. If you can look at the situation and say to yourself, "This is happening, this is reality. I have options." You can leave the company, you can try to change. But just that attitude correction, just that realization, is big.

Once we uncover options for your professional next steps, you'll be in a place to negotiate and find alignment with the company. It puts you in a place of *power*.

YOUR POSSIBLE FUTURE

One of the all-time *worst* interview questions is, "Where do you see yourself in five years?"

It's a shortcut question, to sort you into a category: *Will this person's career goals match up with the organization?* In practice, though, it has the effect of writer's block. I see the same frozen faces of terror with direct reports, or clients, when we approach the subject of their professional dreams.

So let's bring those huge expectations back to Earth a little. For the purposes of this next exercise:

- When we talk about the "future," it means something closer to tomorrow, next week, and next quarter.
- We'll use "prior artifacts"—the careers of other people—so you don't have to start from scratch.
- There are no wrong answers.
- If you're reflecting on your role with open curiosity, you're doing it right.

Find your inspiration

Your first task is to take a look at the professional path of someone you admire.

And before you can object with any of the following "buts":

- "Careers are so fluid, and the tech industry changes so fast!"
- "I admire them, but their careers aren't successful in the traditional sense!"
- "I like parts of their professional path, but not the whole gamut!"

Take what you need as inspiration, and leave the rest. Pretend you're making a Pinterest mood board. We're not copying and pasting every line of someone else's résumé; we're getting a general direction.

To start, select one person whose work is close to yours—maybe they have the same job title, or maybe they work in the same industry. Here are a few sources of inspiration:

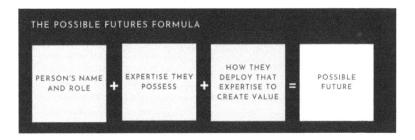

FIG 2.2: The Possible Futures Formula I developed will help you work with "prior art" so that you won't be starting from zero.

- Whose books are on your shelves?
- Whom do you follow on social media or watch on YouTube?
- Whose newsletter do you subscribe to for its resonant insights?
- Whom do you recommend people read, listen to, or think about?
- Whose "vibe" is similar to yours?

If you're still struggling, here's another way to approach this question: name someone you'd want to partner with on a professional project. That's a good shortcut to figuring out whom you respect.

The Possible Futures Formula

Now that you have your inspiration, let's take a look their career arc to help inform yours. The Possible Futures Formula uses the career paths of people you admire to reverse engineer your future role (**FIG 2.2**). To support you through the Possible Futures Formula, I've made a workbook, *Career Planning, without the Pain,* that you can download from fortuna.ink/tools.

To succeed in their role, they have specialized expertise or training. And since possessing expertise is only one piece of the puzzle—we don't earn coin just by *having* knowledge—also take note of how they use that expertise to provide value (**FIG 2.3**).

PERSON'S NAME	EXPERTISE THEY HAVE	HOW THEY CREATE VALUE	THEIR JOB TITLE (AND YOUR POSSIBLE FUTURE)
CLAIRE	BUSINESS PLANNING	ADVISE EARLY-STAGE COMPANIES	CHIEF OPERATING OFFICER
SCOTT	BRAND STRATEGY	BUILDING AN AUDIENCE	PROFESSOR OF BUSINESS
BERNADINE	INDUSTRIAL PROCESSES	WORKFORCE TRAINING	ADVISOR AND CONSULTANT

FIG 2.3: Here are some examples of my (many) professional heroes using the Possible Futures Formula. You can access Career Planning, without the Pain at fortuna.ink/tools.

Using the paths

Keep iterating through this exercise (maybe another two or three times) and then take a step back.

Ask yourself:

- Which job titles or roles come up more than once?
- Which industries do you see represented?
- In what areas do you currently lack expertise?

The paths and skills, on their own, paint a rough picture of the directions your career could take. As you've probably guessed, you'll need to sharpen the picture. Let's get more high-definition by homing in on the details, dimensions, and requirements.

Identify and weigh your priorities

Prioritize the three to five traits that matter most to you in a role. These are your "must-haves": the traits you're willing to make trade-offs for in order to get them. For me, my must-haves are mission-driven work, leaders I admire, autonomy, and working remotely. A colleague I respect values cash money, total compensation, the team, the work she does, and potential for travel.

Mary Moore-Simmons, vice president of engineering at AgentSync, told me that each successive role she has had has helped her clarify her most important criteria. After leading an engineering team at SendGrid during its hypergrowth phase, she wanted more autonomy. She became head of engineering for a new startup, but unfortunately there was no demand for the product. From there, her criteria evolved again. Now, she told me, she's looking for a company "where the culture is healthy, I can create a great environment for my team, and the product is doing well."

Priorities are not static. What was important to me at thirty— being on the road for half the year! Working all the time!— didn't appeal to me at forty: I wanted to be home, chilling with my pug Tuna. Also, the wisdom we gain with each new role shapes our priorities for the next one.

What qualities do you want your role to have? Is there a company size or stage that's most appealing to you? Specific tools that are important? How about remote versus hybrid versus onsite? Does managing people appeal to you? How about maximum coin (100 percent cool if that is your goal—no shame in that game—though there are certainly trade-offs).

Generate a list of three to five criteria for your role, from now-ish to the near future (six months). I recommend you use the Possible Futures Formula in *Career Planning, without the Pain*, since it does the math for you and doesn't limit your space. If you need help brainstorming, check out the list of some common must-haves I've heard from colleagues over the years (FIG 2.4).

Compensation	• Split of cash compensation to equity • Bonus potential • Profit-sharing • Commission structure • Ability to moonlight
Benefits	• Generous leave policies • Per diem • Matching retirement • Learning and development budget • Childcare
Role	• Size of budget • Involves travel / does not involve travel • High profile • Manage people / do not manage people • Large scope of impact • Autonomy • Builds toward next career step • Challenging • Immediate team • Rapport with manager • External collaborators or vendors • Sector or customer you serve • Flexibility of planning your day/week
Company	• Stage of company • Maturity of product or team • Mission-driven • Recognizable brand • Admire leader or leadership team • Remote or onsite

FIG 2.4: Everyone's criteria is different, and determining your must-haves will bring clarity to your decision-making.

Priorities have an aspect of scarcity to them: if everything is a priority, nothing is scarce . You might find it fruitful to brainstorm lots of "must-haves," but settling on three to five will drive clearer decision-making. Remember the boss who wants it fast, cheap, and high-quality? Don't be that guy.

EXAMPLE MUST-HAVES	HOW IMPORTANT IS IT?
MISSION-DRIVEN WORK	9
REMOTE WORK	9
LEADERS I RESPECT	5
AUTONOMY	7
CREATIVITY	3

FIG 2.5: Here's how I would assess my must-haves, assigning each a value between 1 and 10.

Next, we're going to give each of these criteria a weighted value between 1 and 10. I first came across the weighted approach to complex decision-making in Paul Pfleiderer's course, which I highly recommend (https://bkaprt.com/scw48/02-02). Once you look at the criteria in somewhat more objective terms, decisions become easier (FIG 2.5).

As you list your "must-haves" and their weight, are you surprised by any of the criteria or their relative importance? Whenever I do this exercise, I'm shocked at how important "mission-driven" is to me—if there's no mission, the work activities feel rote. I need my actions, however small, to add up to a bigger vision.

Adding it up

In the "Career Composite" section of the workbook, we use some basic math to compare your Possible Futures against one another. This is where the Possible Futures Formula really

CAREER PLANNING, WITHOUT THE PAIN

CAREER COMPOSITE

- FOR EACH POTENTIAL FUTURE ASSESS THE LIKELIHOOD THAT THE ROLE WILL FULFILL YOUR MUST-HAVES.
- USE A 1-10 SCALE, WITH 1 BEING "UNLIKELY" AND 10 BEING "MOST DEFINITELY."
- YOUR CAREER COMPOSITE SCORE SHOULD GIVE YOU SOME STARK INSIGHTS ON HOW THE DIFFERENT ROLES COMPARE TO EACH OTHER.

Your must-haves	Possible Future 1 Chief Operating Officer	Possible Future 2 Professor of Business	Possible Future 3 Advisor and Consultant
Mission-driven work	8	8	3
Remote work	10	1	6
Leadership I admire	9	3	5
Autonomy	10	8	10
Creative colleagues	3	8	3
...			
...			
...			
...			
Score:	286	176	149

FIG 2.6: By creating your "Career Composites," you can compare Possible Futures to one another and see which role has the most potential to meet your criteria. You can access your own copy of *Career Planning, without the Pain* at fortuna.ink/tools.

comes in handy, because we're adding a quantified dimension to help guide your decision-making (FIG 2.6).

In order to get there, we factor your "must-haves" by the likelihood the role will possess them: 1 (not at all) to 10 (definitely). Use your best guess to estimate. That's why we use prior art—do the people you admire, who are in those roles right now, possess those must-haves? (If you know them personally, now would be a good time to ask!)

You'll notice that the workbook encourages you to assign each Possible Future a score. Taken together, those clear, concrete numbers allow you to compare roles. A few questions to ask yourself as you reflect on your scores and Possible Futures:

- Do the scores differ wildly from one another? What does that tell you?
- If scores are close (within a half-dozen points), would you be open to any of those options?
- Did you weigh your must-have's honestly? If you had a set number of points to award for each Possible Future—thirty, say—would those limitations make the differences in your scores more stark?
- What are you willing to do, put up with, or otherwise endure to achieve your "must-haves"?
- Can you improvise and just start doing the job you want?

Keep your highest-scoring Possible Future in mind. You can use it as a template or jumping-off point, whether you are searching for roles or working toward a promotion.

Dealbreakers and "don't-cares"

The Possible Futures Formula focuses on what you *want*, or perhaps what you want *more* of, in a positive sense. But I've also included a tab in the workbook for a category of "Dealbreakers and Don't-Cares"—aspects of work that you want to avoid, have less of in your life, or features of roles that might be important to others, but just aren't for you (**FIG 2.7**).

Personally, I don't care about a glamorous HQ office—I'm never going to go there, and I'd use that capital differently. Leadership coach and former vice president of engineering Lara Hogan finds that, for the leaders she serves, identifying their "don't-cares" is tremendously useful. It gives them permission to ignore criteria that don't matter to them.

Dealbreakers are your boundaries. It's work you would never do, work you would make sacrifices and trade-offs to avoid. A few common examples:

- Tooling—e.g., workflows, programming languages, asynchronous chat
- Cultural norms—e.g., remote work, expectations of travel, stack ranking

DEALBREAKERS AND "DON'T-CARES"

- WHAT ARE YOUR BOUNDARIES? IS THERE WORK THAT YOU WOULD NEVER DO?
- IS THERE A CRITERION THAT LOTS OF PEOPLE CARE ABOUT BUT YOU DON'T?
- ARE THERE ANY ASPECTS ABOUT YOUR CURRENT ROLE THAT AREN'T ALL THAT IMPORTANT TO YOU?

EXAMPLE DEAL-BREAKERS	EXAMPLE "DON'T CARES"
TIMESHEETS	FANCY HQ
STACKED RANKING	LEARNING AND DEVELOPMENT $$
DYNAMIC PRICING	WELL-ESTABLISHED DEPARTMENT

FIG 2.7: Be aware of what you don't want and what you don't care about. This awareness will make your choices more informed. You can access your own workbook at fortuna. ink/tools.

- Business practices—e.g., dynamic pricing, use of cookies, suspicious accounting tactics like WeWork's "community-based EBITA"

Looking through the list of examples, you might find a few to which you are just plain allergic. I have a severe allergy, and it's Microsoft Teams. Nothing makes me feel like I'm in a beige conference room, going over redlines to a mind-numbing contract, like signing into Teams.

Use this list to evaluate new roles, expectations for a potential promotion, or even as a gut check against the company as it changes.

Turning the data into a plan

After filling out the Career Composite section of the *Career Planning, without the Pain* workbook, you'll have a list of skills you need to build. Now it's time to match those with activities that will benefit the business—possibly on a two- to three-year timeline. Think back to Chapter 1 and find out where your company is in its life cycle. Then, consider the likely next steps for the direction of the company:

- Is your function apt to grow, contract, or shift? Is it duplicated in some way?
- Will the company need to expand to new verticals or serve different customers?
- Do you want to manage people? (Or more directly: Does your Possible Future *require* you to have leadership experience?)
- Are you interested in moving to a different department or location?

When to use intuition

Because decision-making can be a bit squishy, I've found that using some quant juice, a little number reasoning, often eases anxiety around complex decisions.

But have you ever made a list of benefits and drawbacks, hated the resulting list, tossed it, and went for the more challenging option anyway? Sometimes when people do this exercise, they still have a strong "Whole Body No" to their highest-scoring Possible Future. That's your intuition talking!

Characteristics of intuition
• It is a cyclical process of thinking associated with the overall cognition of reality
• It is not the opposite of logic
• It is not an irrational action
• It refers to the use of "deeper" knowledge resources collected over a lifetime
• Every person has intuitive potential (but at different levels)
• It is a capability that can be trained and developed
• It participates in any decision-making process
• It uses induction (the conclusion precedes the premises, the whole picture precedes getting to know its parts)
• It is a fast, sometimes even automatic process

Table 1: Characteristics of intuition
Source: own study.

FIG 2.8: Intuition is data—so sayeth peer-reviewed research. (https://bkaprt.com/scw48/02-03, PDF)

Whether you call it a gut instinct, a hunch, or—my personal favorite—"vibes," intuition often gets pitted against logic. If you admit to using your intuition, you're in the realm of glitter Gaia light beams and drum circles. That's not deductive reasoning. That's not logic. That's not *business*.

But here's the thing: we rely on intuition a lot of the time *anyway*. Many of us feel a magnetic pull toward an answer, and use data to back it up after the fact. Kamila Malewska, a scholar at the Poznań University of Economics and Business, found that the more senior an executive, the more they leaned on intuition—which she referred to as "'deeper' knowledge resources collected over a lifetime" (**FIG 2.8**).

If you go through a logical process—taking the time to question your assumptions and biases—and you still have a strong reaction to The Bottom Line, that means there's a "must-have" with an intense weight that you haven't accounted for. What is that thing?

Planning your life isn't a rote task, and it's tough to be "data-driven" when those data points don't exist yet. You may have just produced the first data set as you completed these exercises. Pay attention to any tugs or strong reactions—that is information. All of the data you've collected over the course of your life is Trying To Tell You Something.

ALIGNMENT *IS* NEGOTIATION

Surprise! You're negotiating with your company. In fact, you've *always* been negotiating with your company—negotiating your relationship to it, your role within it, how much effort you invest in it. Many of us have some baggage around the term "negotiation," but I hope to convince you that it's not a bad thing at all.

Alignment is a framework for relating to your organization. In my experience, seeing your relationship to the organization as a dialogue can help break down the fixed points of view that can lead to toxic "us versus them" thinking.

You have the power to accept and integrate the decisions of the company, or step back and follow another path.

At the end of the day, relating to the organization is a kind of negotiation, a kind of partnership. And productive partnerships are all about mutual benefit.

Finding areas of mutual benefit

Mutual benefit is core to Roger Fisher's negotiation process, which he outlined in *Getting to Yes: Getting What You Want without Giving In.* Fisher, during his life as a business professor, negotiation practitioner, and conflict-resolution expert, cofounded the Harvard Negotiation Project in 1979. His bona fides include important roles in peace treaties in Latin America and the Middle East, the resolution of the Iran Hostage Crisis, and the end of apartheid in South Africa. Key to his process was avoiding rigid notions like "driving hard bargains" or zero-sum games—the stuff of night sweats for someone like me.

Instead, he recommended "inventing options for mutual gain." When you approach your manager with a plan from which both of you can gain, the process becomes less heavy, fearful, and driven by loss avoidance.

Put another way, you don't have to exert brute force to get what you want. But you do need to have attractive options, which you've already developed through your Possible Futures and Career Composites exercises.

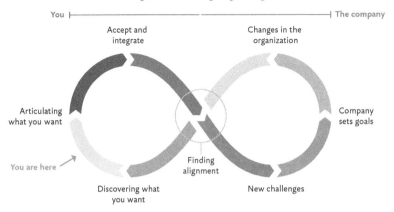

Alignment: an ongoing dialogue

You ├─────────────────── ───────────────────┤ The company

Accept and integrate

Changes in the organization

Articulating what you want

Company sets goals

You are here

Finding alignment

Discovering what you want

New challenges

FIG 2.9: When you look at the organization's goals and compare them to your Possible Futures, do you see any overlap?

Connecting your Possible Future with the company's direction

When GitHub was acquired in 2018, I knew a lot was going to change—this was a shot to take our team to the next level. During the fog of uncertainty, the daily heartbeat of the organization was off. I took some time away from Slack and Zoom to map out how I could weave what I wanted for my career.

In other words, I looked at the changes in the organization, and then invested the time to discover and articulate what my business unit would need in its next phase (**FIG 2.9**).

My plan had three parts:

- The activities my business unit would accomplish
- The results the business could expect to see from those activities
- The skills I'd need to acquire and develop in order to do all of those things

Remember when I said this visioning and planning is the highest-ROI work you can do? This plan evolved into my promotion packet to become a director. Months later, when the opportunity presented itself, I pitched my plan to our CEO. I ended up staying on for another three years. This is the value of knowing what you want: it gives you the ability to jump on opportunities as the company shifts.

If you're able to find alignment between what you want to do and what the business needs, that's power.

SHARING YOUR POSSIBLE FUTURE WITH YOUR MANAGER

It's your manager's job to support your career growth. It's in *their* best interest to invest in you. Their next best alternative is a risk: fighting for a backfill, recruiting candidates, interviewing, negotiating an offer, allotting time for that person to quit their job and onboard, with a few weeks before they can directly contribute. They're looking at *months* of that role sitting empty. Whereas if you present your Possible Future to them, you're taking something off their plate *and* giving them a heads-up about your future plans.

That said, there is *some* risk in sharing your Possible Future with your manager. There are some bad apples out there. You can mitigate this risk with data.

Pay attention to how your manager treats people when they resign

Ask your former colleagues: How did that conversation go? Some tension is fine; it shows that the company values that person and will miss them. If the manager understands and supports this person's career growth, that's a sign that they prioritize the long-term relationship. But if the manager takes it personally, or gets verbally reactive or punishing in their comments, that's not a safe situation. Look for other mentors across the company, or consider pursuing outside opportunities.

Talk to someone your manager has recently promoted

If the company is early-stage or even approaching product / market fit, the manager probably has quite a bit of autonomy in promotion decisions. Find out from your colleague how the manager decided they were ready for promotion, and if your manager was enthusiastic or reticent.

Later in the life cycle, the company will establish career ladders, making the promotion process longer and harder. Managers have to make their case and document it. Insecure managers might hesitate to put their reputation on the line to pitch your promotion. Find out from your colleague if this was the case with their promotion.

Ask your manager: "Where do you see your career going?"

If they open up about their own career ambitions, that bodes well. If they can see past their current role for themselves, they may do the same for you. If they are suspicious or cagey, you might not be able to trust them enough to share your own Possible Future.

If you get a bad feeling from this test balloon, that's a sign. A sign to add "a supportive manager" to your list of criteria in your next role. Abort mission.

If you get positive results, you might lay groundwork for future conversations: "Where do you see this team progressing in the next year? How can my role grow in that process?"

When you say what you want, your manager will either try to find a way to make it happen or tell you that your Possible Future isn't likely in your current role. Either way, you'll have data. And, when it's time to go, you'll have a story that's both honest and expected—you are following your dream.

WHAT'S NEXT: SELLING YOUR IDEAS INTERNALLY

Discovering what you want is tough *internal* work. Now, you need to do the *external* work of communicating those ideas to the decision-makers around you. Let's dig into some strategies that can bring your vision to life.

3 SELLING YOUR IDEAS

I INVITE YOU INTO a common work scenario. Your team is considering changing from an old system to a new one. Whether it's a customer-relationship management system, project management software, observability tooling, or a new language or framework, we've all had to face this problem. You've likely seen two archetypes:

- **The Super Communicator**. This person moves through the organization with ease. The organization fast-tracks her promotions, she lands the most interesting projects, and leaders pick up and use her turns of phrase. Her recommendation for tooling is ultimately adopted.
- **The Idealogue.** This person has a strong point of view that they righteously carry. They frequently come out of meetings feeling frustrated and ignored. Their recommendation for tooling isn't adopted, and this sours their motivation.

Both individuals are smart, competent, and possess enviable expertise. The key difference is that the Super Communicator knows how to sell her ideas, and the Idealogue doesn't. In order

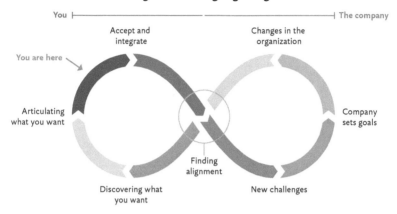

Alignment: an ongoing dialogue

You ├──────────────────────────────────────┤ The company

Accept and integrate

Changes in the organization

You are here

Articulating what you want

Company sets goals

Finding alignment

Discovering what you want

New challenges

FIG 3.1: Articulate what you want in order to align with your company's leaders. This chapter contains tools to help you do that.

to get people to embrace their ideas, Super Communicators have are adept at using these strategies:

- **Analyze the audience.** Find out the professional background, goals, and values of your decision-maker.
- **Package the value.** Showcase the impact you expect to see, making the choice a no-brainer.
- **Surface trade-offs.** Consider other options with their downsides, and underscore the ramifications if people don't implement your idea.

The notion of "selling" might not sit well with you. Fifteen years ago, it sure didn't for me. I'd read job descriptions that included words like "influence," "persuasion," and "clout" and would instantly feel icky. You can think of these strategies as "managing up," but I prefer to think of them as relating to the organization—articulating what you want in a way the organization can hear (**FIG 3.1**).

And here's the thing: one size doesn't fit all. An idea that makes perfect sense to you—in your head—may make a colleague scrunch up their nose and ask "Huh?" From research on both learning styles (https://bkaprt.com/scw48/03-01, PDF) and cognitive recall (https://bkaprt.com/scw48/03-02), we know that people consume information differently depending on context and timing. When you're intentional about whom you are presenting ideas to, and how they prefer to consume information, it's an inclusive act.

And the stakes are high: *if you don't learn how to sell your ideas, you'll limit your reach.* Ideas and initiatives that succeed have momentum. That means others need to buy in to your idea and make it their own. For your ideas to resonate with your boss, VP, or CEO, you need to know what matters to *them*.

AUDIENCE ANALYSIS

When my team worked through their own Possible Futures, they taught me so much about what motivates them. Almost all of them highlighted mission-driven work, but that's where the similarities ended. Some needed more autonomy in their decision-making; others needed clear expectations. As their leader, I was more than happy to oblige.

But it also had the effect of information asymmetry: they didn't know what motivated *me*. After a few projects missed the mark, I asked if they knew their audience. What did they think *I* cared about? The answers were fascinating.

They revealed what they *wished* I cared about, not my actual goals. While that's great feedback for an intentional manager—I could act on their requests—I was setting them up to fail when they took their ideas up the chain. They needed to know what motivates a decision-maker.

Moving forward, I would ask direct reports to think through the following questions about their audience:

- What's their background?
- What motivates them?
- What are the success metrics for their roles?

Study the audience's background

First, find out about the arc of their career. LinkedIn is your friend here. See if you can detect patterns in terms of the size of their previous organizations, areas of focus, or consistent themes in their work history. If their work is varied, they might be a generalist. If it's specialized, you may need to find out more about the domain that matters to them.

Then you can use the data in two important ways.

Tailor your message

Use their background to connect their understanding of the world to your idea. Finding comparisons relevant to their background is always helpful. A colleague of mine worked at NASA, so when we were talking about launching products, we used preflight checklists to ensure consistency. For computer science teachers, we'd relate Git to the data structure of a linked list, something they would recognize.

Infer the impact they want to make on the organization

If they are a product person, they might want to grow the organization through features and technology. Or perhaps they are more of a sales-driven leader, focused on maximizing and extracting value out of a mature offering.

This approach applies both to working with other teams in the organization and to collaborating with peers. When you understand your negotiation partner, your chances of success increase by orders of magnitude.

Consider how they get evaluated

What are your *audience's* incentives? Which numbers does the company expect this person to move? If you're not sure, take a look at their team's key performance indicators, their dashboards, even job descriptions on your company's career site. If your company is mature enough to have career ladders, that's another great source of intelligence about how this person gets measured by the company.

If you're unsure about your audience's goals, their place in the organizational chart will have some info. Line managers often have more operational goals, like feature-level metrics, shipping on schedule, and conversion rates. People that are higher up in the organization have broader goals, like revenue and activation metrics; gross margin for the company; and expansion into new verticals. Remember to keep your audience's place in the organization in mind. I've seen a few presentations fall flat because the presenter was caught up in the weeds of features while pitching to leaders with business-level goals.

Once you have a sense of how they are measured, refer to that goal in your messaging. You're more likely to succeed if you can frame your idea in terms of meeting a joint goal. Here are a few conversation-starters you can use to brainstorm:

- "This will help us both meet a higher margin by... "
- "I saw that you're also looking to lower your turn-around time... "
- "This initiative will meet 27 percent of the company's growth goals."

Suss out their priorities

If you can align your work with what matters to the leader, you'll be more successful. As an example, at DataRobot, vice-president of engineering Chris McDermott told me that his CEO had a "no-process" approach; he thought that if you got rid of red tape, people would get things done. And yet meetings would get bogged down in minutiae and micromanagement. McDermott observed the need for more process, but framed it in a way that suited his CEO's value of autonomy:

> I think part of it was that I aligned myself to the things he cared about, empowering individuals and so on. I would find ways to create the processes that a mature company needs to meet its requirements, but I would do it in a way that made people move faster and got red tape out of the way.

If you're not sure about a leader's priorities, speak to goals surrounding progress and excellence. These are big motivators. For example:

- For a leader who is motivated by progress, describe what you need to work five or ten times faster.
- For a leader who is motivated by excellence, describe how you can you increase customer satisfaction or market dominance.

If you're still not sure about your audience's background, goals, or priorities, listen to the words and phrases they repeat. Consider using those words in your own messaging.

Now let's take what we've gathered—the priorities, the common turns of phrase, the metaphors that will speak to a leader's background—and turn to the output: crafting a successful message.

PACKAGING THE VALUE

Picture your decision-makers in a meeting. Maybe it's in a conference room named something on-brand, like "Thighmaster" or "Inspiration Station." Everyone sitting in well-designed chairs, ready for Serious Business. Or maybe you're remote, so your leaders are little tiles in a Zoom call.

What, in your imagination, are they talking *about*?

In my experience, leadership meetings have two core activities: weighing proposed solutions, and making decisions. Your company has hired smart people, and those smart people make the case that we should focus on performance, or growth, or market share, depending on their role.

How do you make your idea stand out from the rest? How do you present your idea in a way that makes it easy for leadership to say yes? Here's how:

- Use the Pain, Dream, Fix framework to make your story-telling airtight.

- Make the user badass—focus on what superpower your idea will unlock.
- Surface the trade-offs—highlight what you're giving up and what's at stake.

Pain, Dream, Fix

Decision-makers don't have a lot of time, so don't waste it with a messy message. A few common messy-message offenders:

- **Navel-gazing.** When you start with "Today, we're so excited to announce" or "We are thrilled to introduce" or "I'm excited to show off," that messaging makes the idea about *you*. It's great that you're excited—but why should the audience care?
- **Going too deep.** Experts who are really close to a project can use way too much detail. They care so much about the project that their pitch becomes about *them* rather than the project's value to the organization. Does your audience care about UI details or a context-rich historical background? Keep your message short and high-level. You can always dig deeper if you get questions.
- **Being too vague.** Phrases like "We'll make something great," "Modern tooling, the way it should be," "Launch something amazing," have all the tangibility of vapor. What is the decision-maker saying "yes" or "no" to, exactly? Show them a clear problem and a concrete solution.

To boil down messy messaging into quick, clear points, I use the Pain, Dream, Fix framework I learned from business leaders and educators Alex Hillman and Amy Hoy (https://bkaprt.com/scw48/03-03). Pain, Dream, Fix looks at three anchor points for your messaging:

- **Pain:** Describe the problem in a way that homes in on the pain your *customer*, *audience*, or *company* experiences.
- **Dream:** Next, narrate what the same situation would look like if you dissolved that pain. Would it be easier, faster, smoother?

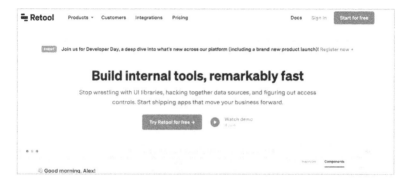

FIG 3.2: Retool's homepage quickly addresses the Pain, Dream, and Fix for its audience.

- **Fix:** Once your audience is primed and in that problem space with you, introduce your proposal. It could be a product, a service, or an idea.

Let's start by applying the Pain, Dream, Fix framework to an area we can recognize: landing page taglines. These top-level messages tightly focus on the pain the user feels, achieving the dream with the fix the product offers.

The first example is Retool (**FIG 3.2**). It's pretty common for teams other than engineering to have technical needs. Marketing may need to capture data, respond to customers, or implement SEO workflows. Operations may need to build MVP logistics tools, track supply-chain needs, or follow contracts. But building those tools isn't the core focus of the business, so they are unlikely to get any significant dev time on the technical roadmap.

Retool directly responds to this pain on their homepage:

- **Pain:** Building internal tools is tough.
- **Dream:** What if you could build the tools your business needs, easily and quickly?
- **Fix:** Retool is the product that will help you build internal tools quickly.

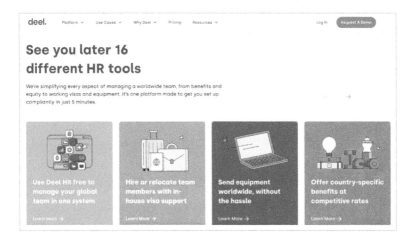

FIG 3.3: Deel offers approachable HR tools geared toward resolving pain points for its customers.

If you have employees in different states (or different countries), managing each nexus, complying with the payroll requirements of each region, and navigating employment regulations is a high operational overhead. Deel has a suite of tools that speaks to those exact pain points for companies (**FIG 3.3**):

- **Pain:** Managing a global team imposes a heavy HR load.
- **Dream:** What if you could use one tool instead of sixteen?
- **Fix:** Deel provides an "end to end" solution.

Once you can spot Pain, Dream, Fix "in the wild," you'll see it everywhere—especially in infomercials, commercials, and ads.

Next, let's apply Pain, Dream, Fix to a few work scenarios. You probably hear "messy messaging" all the time—going too deep, navel-gazing, and being too vague are all examples of "asks" that don't clearly package value.

Since the audience here consists of decision-makers, focus on the pain the *company* feels (not you) in quantitative terms of time, capability, and capital. Then, describe what the results of your proposal will look like, and their impact. Finally, usher

MESSY MESSAGING	PAIN	DREAM	FIX	CLEAR MESSAGING
We'd like to implement Salesforce; everyone agrees it's the tool they prefer.	We missed 26 leads last week because we're managing them in a spreadsheet.	We can increase sales efficiency by 150%...	...by using a CRM.	We missed 26 leads last week because we're managing them in a spreadsheet. We can increase sales efficiency with a CRM.
This program needs someone to run it, so I've asked for an additional head count. We could do some amazing things in this market.	There are 1,381 open support requests.	We could capture an additional 5 percent of market share...	...with an additional new role.	This customer segment is currently underserved—there are 1,381 open support requests. We could capture an additional 5 percent of market share with one additional new role.
I don't want to work on that project. The developer experience stinks, and it goes down all the time.	Our last outage cost $1.2M in lost revenue.	We could boost reliability by 23 percent...	with a rewrite of this area of the codebase.	Our last outage cost $1.2M in lost revenue. We could boost reliability by 23 percent with a rewrite.

FIG 3·4: Three examples of messy messaging made clearer through the Pain, Dream, Fix framework.

in your solution as an obvious solve. It's a recipe for an airtight message that's easy to parse (**FIG 3.4**).

Make the user badass

Walk through the electronics section in any "big box" store in North America, and you'll be surrounded by screens telling you what makes them special. This television has this many dots per inch, this one has surround sound, that one turns into an electronic photo frame. They are all selling *features* of a television. As a result, you really can't tell them apart. They are commodities, without much emotional connection.

Now remember the first time you walked into an Apple store. You were greeted by a "genius" helping you *unlock super-powers* with their product. As a further example, one recent campaign used only photos that users took with their iPhones. Their message isn't about the components of the screen, or the camera—Apple helps its users become *better photographers*.

This is Kathy Sierra's rallying cry: we need to make the user "a badass" in their domain. Sierra, a luminary in the fields of design, marketing, technical education and cofounder of the Head Start book series, points out that as product people, we tend to focus on the components of our work. *We* care about those, but the user really doesn't.

Users don't want to simply use your product—they want to become better, more of an expert, more badass, and your product helps them do that. Sierra spells it out in her book *Badass: Making Users Awesome* (https://bkaprt.com/scw48/03-04):

> They don't want to be badass at our thing.
> They want to be badass at what they do.
> **They want badass** results.

We can apply her lessons about marketing to how you sell your ideas at work. Think about your last idea to change something, or do something new. Did you pitch your idea in terms of the components—the nuts and bolts of the thing—or did you focus on the results?

Decision-makers want results too. A few winning approaches are:

- Increasing the capacity or efficiency of the organization as a whole
- Growing in terms of user base, sales, activation
- Decreasing friction, lag, loss to competition

You might choose to support your pitch with data, or with concrete examples. But start with the superpower that would be unlocked.

Surface the trade-offs

Leaders are always making trade-offs, weighing short- and long-term gains and risks. But decisions that seem clear at the CEO or VP level can get murky when they permeate your work. I remember when a leader really wanted to focus on quality. Did their expectation for excellence trump speed? Did it trump user acquisition? It wasn't clear to me until I asked. Once I knew the implications of their decisions, I could, in turn, make my own decisions.

Neha Batra, vice president of engineering at GitHub told me she uses a tactic called "closing the loop." In her experience, leaders don't necessarily feel the effects of their decisions. There's a gap, an incomplete loop, since leaders can't possibly see all of the implications of their actions. When we surface those trade-offs via feedback and data, that's closing the loop.

Batra remembers a very intense standing meeting that took her ten hours to prepare for each week. Her leadership got what they needed from that meeting, so they didn't have any problems with it. She knew what motivated that leader—efficiency and autonomy—so she closed the loop by surfacing the trade-offs she was making in terms that her leadership understood.

I framed my request in terms of efficiency and autonomy—"Hey, I'm spending ten hours a week on this meeting, which keeps me from actually working on the product. How should we proceed now?" They never wanted me to spend ten hours on this meeting. Now that they have this information, they have a choice to make. What I'm trying to do here is close the loop—give them a wider understanding of their decisions and a clearer choice. The only way to close the loop is to give them more context.

When Neha makes her trade-offs clear, her leader gets a more complete picture. When you use this tactic, pay attention to the effect your feedback has. Does your leader change their expectations?

SELLING YOUR POSSIBLE FUTURE

You now know how to make a compelling business case to decision-makers. All of these skills will assist you in bringing your Possible Future to life. Whom will you need to collaborate with if you want to grow in your role? They're your audience. How would you pitch your Possible Future to a decision-maker? Ask yourself:

- Does your Possible Future match your audience's priorities?
- In what ways could your Possible Future help your audience reach their goals?
- What pain does your role fix?
- How would your Possible Future make the organization more badass?
- What's the cost to the organization if it doesn't support your Possible Future?

Once you have your answers, you can make your case.

WHAT'S NEXT: TIMING AND TURNOVER

You've spent all this time understanding your leader, building trust with them, finding out what makes them tick. But one day you receive an email with a subject line like "Farewell!" or "Moving on" and you panic—another period of change, more unknowns. Leadership changes offer the perfect time to use your new super-communicator skills. The next chapter will show you why.

4

COPING WITH LEADERSHIP CHANGES

MANY MOONS AGO, I received the dreaded Slack message from my manager.

"Can you talk—today?"

Warily entering the Google Hangout (this was pre-Zoom), I saw both cofounders sitting in an otherwise empty conference room. They broke the news—they were going their separate ways—and the cofounder I reported to would be moving on. In retrospect, they handled it respectfully and honestly, and I can now admire them for how they comported themselves amid what I'm sure was smoldering ball of tension.

But at that moment, young Vanessa was *terrified*.

If I could go back in time, I'd tell young Vanessa to seize the opportunity. Go connect with the remaining founder, find areas of common ground, talk about where I wanted to take the role, and not to take it personally if it wasn't a fit. The experience shook me up and took months to recover from. After this first drastic leadership change, though, I was more prepared.

It's easy to get swept up in the ambient panic surrounding leadership changes. There's a communication vacuum while the company formally shakes out the details, and information moves across teams at different velocities. The situation is fraught with gossip and worst-case-scenario assumptions.

Psychologist Tara Brach tells one of my favorite jokes about change and anxiety: a son sends his mom a telegram with the message, "Start worrying. Details to follow" (https://bkaprt. com/scw48/04-01). The joke underscores how "useful" worrying really is, that we default to worrying when we don't even know what we're worrying *about*.

The lack of clarity can send employees into a sort of personal austerity mode, putting off purchases or experiences that might bring them joy or calm. Some folks describe the sensation of their life being put on hold until they know where the company is headed. Fear drives this sort of thinking, with the underlying alarm being: "What will this mean for me?"

This chapter will offer an alternative way to approach leadership changes, which can happen frequently throughout a company's life cycle. As a result, you'll have a plan in place to make the most of the next big change. This chapter walks you through how to:

- Anticipate changes in leadership at inflection points for the company
- Analyze what problem the leadership change is attempting to solve
- Use the ensuing period of experimentation to pitch your ideas
- Find ways to align with the new direction that meet your goals
- Develop strategies to adapt to the company's new iteration

Imagine the next time you hear your boss or CEO is leaving—and feeling curiosity and potential instead of panic. Some of the biggest opportunities to make an impact, bring about your vision, and negotiate with the company come during these periods.

ANTICIPATING CHANGES IN LEADERSHIP

Few events shake up a company as much as leadership turnover. And yet it's shockingly common. To take the company from hypergrowth to exit, for example, investors and the wider board of directors may demand a more experienced operator scale to the company. *Harvard Business Review* says somewhere between 20 and 40 percent of startup founders move on "at the behest of investors" (https://bkaprt.com/scw48/04-02).

Leadership changes can come in a few guises:

- The CEO gets replaced.
- Your direct manager moves on.
- The department head leaves.
- New specialized leaders come onboard as the organization grows.
- Reorganizations shuffle your company into a new structure.
- An acquisition or merger takes place.

Usually, these changes come about when one part of the organization (or more!) isn't functioning optimally. There's a blockage somewhere, and new leaders get deployed to fix it. It's like the classic "what got you here won't get you there" adage: a leadership change is a reboot. The reboot is an opportunity to determine where the resources need to flow next. As a personal example, when GitHub was acquired, my sense was that the organization had gone as far as it could go in its current configuration. We needed new product vision and leadership in order to compete.

The same thinking goes for leadership roles for the hypergrowth organization: the company needs leaders with different skills at different phases of maturity. Veteran HR executive Deva Santiago, head of talent acquisition at Tailscale and an early hire at Dropbox, told me she advises employees to expect these shifts in leadership as a company's strategy shifts from early days to sustained success. Sometimes leaders reach the edge of their abilities, and a new leader gets "layered" above them:

Sometimes early hires are not going to be the ones to scale their teams. You may hire a leader to run sales, who may be great at zero to 20 million in annual recurring revenue. But you may have to think about layering that person later on. So as an employee, you can understand in which stages and phases these things happen.

At the same time, if your organization is going through a period of growth, the company might hire new leaders to staff more specialized positions. All this evidence points to a pretty predictable conclusion: you will likely have a new leader in the very near term.

To the best of your ability, find out why the organization is changing leadership. This new leader is filling a gap. It could be for a host of reasons, like expansion, expertise, or maturity of the company. If you see opportunity for mutual gain with this new leadership, a way to bring your goals and theirs together, now is the time to experiment.

A CHANGE IS A TERRIBLE THING TO WASTE

David C. Baker calls these types of reboot phases "rip the Band-Aid off" periods—there is so much change afoot that leaders and individual contributors alike are reconsidering how things should work. Employees at every level are primed for change, and even the most conservative organizations are open to doing things differently. He characterizes these Band-Aid phases as times when:

- *There's already loads of disruption and there's no equilibrium that we are trying to maintain.*
- *There's a larger "cover" for your decisions; a way to explain or justify the actions. (https://bkaprt.com/scw48/04-03)*

Since you have a plan for your role, you can consider this a period of wider experimentation, or of altering a process that isn't working. Mine the org chart for additional opportunities.

As an example, when Tilde Ann Thurium was an engineer at Pinterest, they were dissatisfied with the limited gender selections in the sign-up flow. During a reorganization and an ensuing period of disorganized code ownership, they were able to develop and ship the option to make your gender an emoji, or a combination of emoji (https://bkaprt.com/scw48/04-04, video).

There is plasticity and slack in the goals, processes, and staffing here—use it to mold the outcome you want. It's the perfect time to pitch your ideal role to your manager or area leader. Like the common patterns in organizations we discussed in Chapter 1, a leadership change also has a pretty consistent arc. Those patterns give us the information that can inform our next step.

A LEADER'S FIRST NINETY DAYS

When a new leader joins an organization, the clock starts: they have ninety days to make an impact and show tangible progression toward their goals. Leaders take predictable steps during this period, and their decisions will tell you a lot about the kind of leader they plan to be. Let's take a look at the common actions you'll see leaders take, and what you can learn from them.

They will set organization-wide goals

Leaders have gathered data about the organization, spent time analyzing and interpreting it, and will use those insights to set their vision and strategy.

When GitHub got a new CEO, he introduced us to what he referred to as "The Core Four"—four top-level metrics that all our activities should contribute to. I saw that our team's student outreach goals could align with the organization's focus on growing an active user base. I knew which numbers we were trying to move from x to y and how to present our goals in terms of moving those four metrics. To me, this provided instant clarity in terms of how I should talk about our mission and pitch our business-planning activities.

These new goals and your previous goals may diverge—ask your leader about that difference, so that they can provide clarity.

If they don't clearly define the goals, listen for repeated phrases. Not all leaders are gifted communicators. For example, "frugality" might mean greenlighting initiatives that reduce cost. "Speed" might shape your presentations in terms of efficiency.

They will meet people to inspire the team and build trust

When a leader sets a high-level vision for the company, they are making an offer *to you*. They're selling you their vision—the company will only be able to accomplish those goals with *your* effort and genius. The organization has to buy in to the vision, since achieving those goals often means sacrifice or tough times ahead.

The leader will probably "socialize" their plans, or go on a road show to different teams within the company. They may meet with individuals to get their take on the vision, and to show the organization that they're a real person. Former GitHub COO Erica Brescia told me that in her first few weeks on the job, she had seventy one-on-one meetings. *Seventy.* These meetings are an excellent way to find out what those goals mean for you, and for you to share your vision for your role.

Sell your story with a deck or a document

I first met Brescia when she was on her listening tour as GitHub's COO, taking the organization's pulse and gathering feedback. She asked pointed questions, and I wondered to myself, "Geez, we're like one of dozens of teams she needs to get her arms around. How is she keeping all of this information *in her head?*"

The pro move here: show up with documentation or a deck. When a team gets a new leader, they're taking in a lot of information at once—make the most of your time with them by clearly articulating how you work. In our interview, she shared her advice on how to set yourself up for success with new leadership:

You're much better off coming in prepared. Be clear and write it down. Bring attention to anything urgent. Tell your leader how your organization functions. If you're an individual contributor, help the leader understand the work that you do, and if anything needs improvement, be ready with suggestions.

When she remembers the seventy one-on-ones she had in the first few weeks of the job, those who came in prepared still stand out to her. "They set us up for making decisions for the organization right away."

Highlight your best "bright spot"

As new leaders get to know new organizations, they will gravitate toward—and invest in—areas that are working. Chip and Dan Heath call these "bright spots" (https://bkaprt.com/scw48/04-05). They advise leaders to find out what's working in their organization and to do more of it. Bright spots can be feedback tactics, lightweight interventions that make a big impact, or the way decisions are made—any process that is "homegrown" as part of the DNA of the organization.

Shining a light on these areas shows that the leaders trust employees—they aren't importing solutions from elsewhere—and the stories are usually pretty darn inspirational.

Start thinking about what stories you can tell to illustrate that your team, feature, or project is a bright spot. I like to keep a few of those stories in a notes document, and add to them over time. That way, when you come across a decision-maker or new leader, you can reference those "bright spots."

Leaders are people

Each individual leader, down to your own manager, may be going through their own "stuff." Their brain has limits too. I spoke to an executive who said that she always notices when employees approach leaders with empathy, rather than their own self-interest:

> People can default to tunnel vision—"What does this mean for me?" I don't know if that serves you very well. Have empathy for a leader that may have a lot of learning to do, and may have their own anxiety about the role.

One skill here is taking a leader's temperature at the outset to find out what their mood, approach, or early thinking is about a given topic. If they aren't in the same space as you, not receptive to collaboration or making decisions, the meeting can go awry. You can start the meeting by asking some general, open questions:

- What are you thinking about head count?
- Are you in a space to walk through the budget?
- What's the climate around planning? If I had a plan for Q3, would that be too early?

Also, tying your work to shared goals can go a long way. You both want the company to succeed, so referencing their high-level goals and pitching your ideas in those terms can help your conversation to be productive.

They might clean house

There's no way to sugarcoat this—the decisions about who will stay or go after a leadership turnover often happen within the first sixty days. Depending on the health of the business when the CEO joins, involuntary attrition (terminations) can range from 12.5 to 26 percent (https://bkaprt.com/scw48/04-06).

With a new vision, leaders may bring with them their own crew of trusted experts, especially at the leadership level. They may wish to eliminate cultural debt (practices, processes, and policies that don't work), address role duplication, or change course from an outdated strategy. Top-level announcements might give you early cues. Or they might not.

When telling me about his time with an early-stage tech company, Graham Neray recalled a new CEO who came in and laid off employees:

> When the new CEO came in, he terminated a lot of the sales people and made significant pricing changes immediately. It was clear from day one that he was making decisions about the company's direction.

If you're one of the ones left standing, analyze the choices your leader has made. Neray deduced that his new CEO was decisive and had strong opinions about how the product should be packaged and sold.

Being laid off

If you're one of the ones getting laid off, I feel you and I feel for you. The shame of a layoff can feel so haunting, and knowing it happens frequently in early-stage tech organizations doesn't make it easier.

When I got laid off, I wish I had had:

- The confidence to share with my network that I needed help finding my next gig. When I see folks sharing that they've been laid off on LinkedIn or Twitter, I respect the resolve it takes to overcome the shame associated with a layoff. I also want to help them!
- The knowledge gleaned from Pam Selle's book *Beyond the Résumé* (https://bkaprt.com/scw48/04-07). The TL;DR: proactively tell people what you're looking for, and you'll be top of mind when a role comes up (https://bkaprt.com/scw48/04-08).
- The perspective of Zen monk Pema Chodron, specifically from *When Things Fall Apart*. Her insights bring more calm and reduce strife after any major setback (https://bkaprt.com/scw48/04-09).

For me, the immediate shock took some time to pass. Then there was a frenetic period of trying to change the painful spot I found myself in—applying for tons of jobs, taking lots of meetings.

In the end, what was most useful was stepping back and asking myself what the role had taught me: about the kind of work I wanted to do, about the kind of organization I wanted to work with. My Possible Futures thinking came out of that period, and you may find it useful to revisit that plan.

After a round of layoffs

Change is pain, and nowhere is that more evident than in mass layoffs. They leave a huge emotional dent in an organization, which needs to heal to move forward. Let's spend some time addressing that grief, because companies don't often address the emotional upheaval that their change brings about.

HEALING FROM CHANGE

A mass layoff is a traumatic change to the organization. The employees left have pain and guilt to process. Some organizational scholars call the remaining employees "survivors," and draw corollaries to it from established research on grief (https:// bkaprt.com/scw48/04-10).

Processing "organizational grief"

If grief has touched your life, you know that working through loss doesn't happen overnight. And the larger the change, the larger the "blast radius" on the organization. Good leaders understand that there's an adjustment period, and make space for employees to come to terms with new decisions. Ida Benedetto, organizational change director for the consulting firm NOBL, told me:

> *Change is loss. Even if it's a positive change. Even if you are aligned with the direction the company is going in, there's still loss in that change. Conversely, when a colleague is departing, for whatever reason, there's a loss there, especially if you had*

a positive relationship or even just a solid working relationship. There's upset, uncertainty in how you might get your work done without that person, or what it might look like when somebody else steps in.

NOBL has built on the work of Dr. Rosabeth Moss Kanter to help explain why, even if your role is mostly unaffected, the change might hit you right in the feels (https://bkaprt.com/scw48/04-11, PDF). Kanter identified several concrete drivers of those strong feelings:

- **Loss of control**: autonomy is a prime driver for many people, so changes that rattle their sense of control will trigger a strong response.
- **Excess uncertainty**: no one likes to be waiting for more details to firm up.
- **Surprise, surprise**: with a shocking decision or news, people react defensively.
- **The "Difference Effect"**: many find support in consistency and routine, and they don't want that disturbed by doing things differently.
- **Loss of face**: people may interpret change as a critique of their work, or as failure.
- **Concerns about future competence**: people might panic about whether they'll be good enough in this new realm, with new tools and new ways of doing things.
- **Ripple effects**: one decision may displace what you were working on, what team you're on, or what kind of work you do.
- **More work**: some people are motivated by new things and by innovation, and are willing to burn the midnight oil to get there. Some aren't. Change does often mean revising, adapting, and learning new ways of working—and that takes more time.
- **Past resentment**: sometimes changes can kick up bad blood that's been roiling for a while. This change plus the cumulative effect of past actions can be the last straw for some.
- **A real threat**: change can affect our livelihoods. More on that in a bit.

Change also affects pieces of the organization differently. In Neray's example, the sales organization might have felt a loss of face, while marketing perhaps suffered more of what Kanter calls a "difference effect" because new pricing translates to new processes. But it all hurts.

Belief grief

For pre-exit tech companies in particular, when the company changes, you're likely going to be hit hard by a shift in *identity*. You believed the company was mission-driven, and the outcomes of the layoffs are in direct opposition to the mission. Maybe you believed that your leaders would never make this choice.

Social psychologist Dolly Chugh uses the term "belief grief" to describe a pattern that emerges when we're faced with evidence that our closely held beliefs about ourselves aren't true (https://bkaprt.com/scw48/04-12). Denial, outrage, bargaining, depression, acceptance—many (if not all) of these stages apply to losing our beliefs as well. Many of us identify closely with our company, and big changes open up the need to grieve our previous beliefs about it.

It's unlikely the company will remain the idealistic, mission-focused, "change the world" organization you joined. This was especially true for my team at GitHub, and the heartbreak was real. I remember the day the deal closed. We'd been expecting it for six months. It was good change, we knew it was coming, but it was hard to let go of the thing we loved.

Helpful rituals

We have rituals to anchor the phases of our lives and holidays to mark the cycle of the seasons, but astoundingly few rituals to mark the phases of a company.

The rhythm of "moving fast" leaves little time to pause, reflect, and close the book on a previous version of the team. *Maybe* when a teammate leaves, you throw a party that celebrates their contribution. This allows the team to process its grief.

After a significant change, like a mass layoff, you need somewhere to mourn together. Maybe it's a dinner, or a happy hour where everyone shares a memory, or taking a group photo, or watching a movie as a team just to share space (one of my colleagues swears by Clue).

Or, if you're able stomach some whimsy, you might participate in what Kursat Ozenc and Margaret Hagan from the Stanford d.school call a "Funeral for the Bygone" in their book *Rituals for Work*.

> The Funeral for the Bygone is a ceremony to let people recognize, honor, and celebrate what is being left behind and the many people who had worked so hard on it. It is also a way to mark the changeover from this old way of working or this former team structure. The funeral can be a clear point of transition, by which people know that they are in a different era now. *(https://bkaprt.com/scw48/04-13)*

Mourning rituals exist for a reason. Sharing space with others who also experienced what was special about the organization will help you close the book on that chapter.

THE NEXT PHASE

A company-wide reboot creates space for you to pause and reflect on your role—take it. No matter your function, your role will be different now: you'll relate to leaders differently, you may even explain your work differently. At a high level, you have two choices:

· Accept this next phase of the company
· Take a step back and find another venue for your talents

Accept and integrate

Once you've worked through the grief that comes up, ask yourself if you can say yes to the company's next phase. Accepting this new iteration of the company is a deeply personal decision.

FIG 4.1: Accepting and integrating means saying yes to the organization in its next phase.

It means shedding your expectations of the way the company used to be, not trying to force the company back in time, and being open to the new organization's needs (FIG 4.1). A few prompts to jump-start your reevaluation:

- From 1 (not at all) to 10 (totally happening), what is the likelihood of you achieving your Possible Future with *this iteration* of the organization?
- Whom do I need to connect with, both within and outside the organization, to make my Possible Future a reality?

To get Zen for a moment, "acceptance" does not mean "approval." Buddhist monk and scholar Pema Chodron makes this distinction:

> Accepting something, by the way, isn't the same as liking it. To accept a feeling that we habitually associate with discomfort doesn't mean we immediately turn around and start enjoying it. It means being okay with it as part of the texture of human life. (*https://bkaprt.com/scw48/04-14*)

Acceptance also takes time. When I realized that Microsoft was a bigger, stronger organization than GitHub, and that their presence would deeply influence GitHub's future, it took me a minute to digest that (FIG 4.1).

Stepping back

If you don't want to go where the company is going, it's time to redirect your efforts. You aren't alone: surviving employees face more work and reduced budgets. Big, traumatic changes like mass layoffs tend to make high-value employees leave (https:// bkaprt.com/scw48/04-10, subscription required). If you sense that you're headed that way, there are tools to help you move on at end of this book.

YOUR TOOLSET FOR WHAT'S NEXT

Deciding whether to accept and integrate or step back is a practice, an ongoing conversation—a sort of living compass. When big changes arise in company culture, that habit will not only be useful to give you perspective; it will also lessen the impact of each successive change. Next, we'll take a look at the things that change as an organization grows.

5 CULTURE SHOCK

IN 1956, ANTHROPOLOGIST Horace Mitchell Miner published his classic essay about the peculiarities of a people who inhabited North America (and were incidentally obsessed with cleanliness). It began:

> " Professor Linton first brought the ritual of the Nacirema to the attention of anthropologists twenty years ago, but the culture of this people is still very poorly understood. They are a North American group living in the territory between the Canadian Cree, the Yaqui and Tarahumare of Mexico, and the Carib and Arawak of the Antilles. Little is known of their origin, although tradition states that they came from the east. According to Nacirema mythology, their nation was originated by a culture hero, Notgnihsaw, who is otherwise known for two great feats of strength—the throwing of a piece of wampum across the river Pa-To-Mac and the chopping down of a cherry tree in which the Spirit of Truth resided.
> —HORACE MITCHELL MINER, BODY RITUAL AMONG THE NACIREMA (https://bkaprt.com/scw48/05-01)

Written in the style of an ethnography or a monograph, his framing of the Nacirema— "American" spelled backward—puts some distance between us, as observers, and a culture we barely see. After all, if it's the water we swim in, how can we see it objectively?

The same is true for our work culture; it's hard to look at objectively. Ask five different tech employees to define "work culture," and you'll get five different answers. Sometimes the definition comes into clearer focus only *in comparison with something else*: Is your culture more or less hierarchical than Amazon? More or less creative than Etsy? And so on.

At a high level, culture is:

- a way of working (e.g., your tools, the expectations the company has for you)
- shared by a group of people (e.g., ways of collaborating, the structure of teams, access, decision-making)
- at a particular point in time.

When the organization lurches in another direction at significant clip, that's when you're going to get culture shock.

We covered the life cycle of a high-growth organization in Chapter 1. Every six months or so, take a step back and compare the culture of the organization *when you joined* to *how it works now*. Try to view it with the detached neutrality of a BBC nature documentary. ("In the wild, a handful of tech workers concurrently are typing... ")

The demand for growth will make the culture change faster than you can recognize. When scaling systems and new challenges surface, goals for growth grow broader, and the organization's structure shifts (FIG 5.1). Processes will emerge and take hold, possibly without you noticing. New hire class after new hire class will come online, get onboarded, and start making decisions before you even know their names.

The commitments that the organization has made to you, as an employee, are a moving target. Larger, more mature companies have built-in inflection points, quarterly goals, or halves of the year ("H1, H2") where teams assess what has changed. But for earlier-stage organizations, you've got to make those

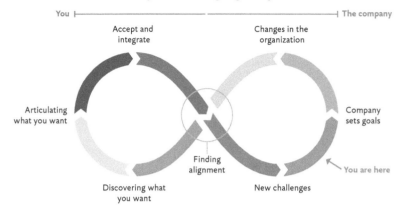

Alignment: an ongoing dialogue

You ├────────────────────────────────────┤ The company

Accept and integrate

Changes in the organization

Articulating what you want

Company sets goals

Finding alignment

You are here

Discovering what you want

New challenges

FIG 5.1: The demands of scale introduce new challenges to an organization. Before the company has a chance to set and fund new goals, there's a messiness, a chaotic period where policies, processes, and practices no longer work.

inflection points yourself, because every six months or so, the target moves again—you'll need to rethink expectations, policies, and norms. Managers begin to grapple with the "that's not fair" complaint:

- "What do you mean, I can't go on sabbatical? We offered one six months ago!"
- "We don't do signing bonuses anymore? Jeff got his and he's the newest team member!"
- "But my city was a Zone 1 for location-based pay last year!"

Things that may once have been true no longer are. Welcome to the hyper-growth phase of the life cycle.

GROWING PAINS

Culture is the hardest thing to hold on to as an organization grows—this came up time and again in research, anecdotes, and in my own experience leading a team through change. Not every leader is culture-focused, so the culture drifts without anyone really noticing. And, after a certain point, the organization can take on a life of its own. As the company scales, the demands of growth will bring about:

- **Hiring sprees:** new employees are added at speed.
- **Office expansion:** the company creates a footprint in a new location or country.
- **Elevated product expectations:** the product matures into a business-critical tool.
- **Standard operating procedures:** established workflows replace improvising.
- **Role specialization:** departments and functions get formalized (and siloed).
- **Selective information-sharing:** instead of radical transparency, the company shifts toward sharing information strategically.
- **Security review:** —once people want your product, the company must take measures to protect it.

Each of these actions has consequences that will affect you. This chapter will walk through the common indicators that your culture is changing.

New people, new culture

How much your organization will grow depends on its industry and business type. For high-growth organizations, doubling in size every year is pretty common, especially near rounds of funding. Deva Santiago, the vice president of people at Tailscale, told me:

> *All of a sudden, you hit a growth phase and you need to add twenty more features and thirty more salespeople. Something's going to give. You won't be completely aligned.*

When you parachute in dozens or hundreds of people at a time, the culture shifts. Each new employee who walks in the door doesn't have your shared history with the organization. They don't "just know" your values automatically. What's more, they probably have their own ideas about How Things Should Be Done, especially if they're in a leadership role. Leaders usually model and uphold the values of a company; in a way, they are concentrated "flavor bombs" of culture in an organization. If a bunch of new ones come in with different values, that can shift the culture considerably.

Consulting firm BCG has studied the culture clash that can occur during mergers and acquisitions, when organizations import and absorb new employees essentially overnight. BCG's "integration teams" have the heavy job of weaving together two (often disparate) cultures. Even when two companies come from altogether different countries, with entirely different languages, religious traditions, and government structures, the differences in *company* culture are the starkest:

> *Culture is more a function of company than of country. In 80% of the deals examined, we found marked differences between a company's divisions within the same country. The higher up in the ranks, the greater the differences. In most dimensions, senior managers showed differences two to three times greater than nonmanagers. (https://bkaprt.com/scw48/05-02)*

Leaders transmit culture through their teams' policies, tools, and norms. The more people who join an organization at once, the faster culture can change. The problem becomes amplified when new offices open.

Regional or international expansion

During the acquisition "quiet period," one of my goals was to expand our team's activities to India and China. While we were small, that was just a dream. But with Microsoft behind us, it was a different story. I couldn't wait to meet students in Bangalore and Chengdu to see how computer science was taught. When I learned our COO was focused on international expansion, I did my level best to get on her calendar.

As new offices sprang up, a palpable difference in culture emerged. People started to refer to our San Francisco office as "Corporate HQ"—an entity that we needed to consult for the ultimate decision. I would think to myself, "GitHub? Corporate? Really?" Their expectation of a corporate overlord must have come from *somewhere*—new employees from larger organizations, global teams with regional reporting structures; I can't be sure. But I was conscious of this shift from a distributed team, to an "us versus them" notion of regional offices and HQ.

I loved working with our India team, and learned so much from them. But some on our US-based team were apprehensive about the eight-hour time difference. Would they need to shift their lifestyles and working hours? What about the flexibility they had previously enjoyed in their workday? As Santiago continued to tell me about her experience, she emphasized that this sort of inflection point happens every time global teams require more structure:

> *Say you started in this remote environment but now you hired in Europe and India, and you can't have entirely flexible hours because you do need some sync. You just broke your entire culture. Now you've broken a commitment you told all these early employees, early on.*

As the company transitions to specialized regions, opens new offices, or even just welcomes an influx of global employees, a particular kind of heartbreak needs to be addressed. The shared understanding of the culture is changing, in this case around identity and process. It's also around this time that the company will make key choices about their organizational design. Get ready for org chart musical chairs.

Reading the org chart

If your company expands globally, they'll usually follow one of two structural patterns: functional structure, or divisional structure. This means that your organizational chart will change, and you may find yourself sitting closer or farther away from top

FIG 5.2: In a functional organization, you'll be grouped with folks who do similar work to you, perhaps globally.

decision-makers as a result. Let's take a look at these structures and weigh their benefits and drawbacks.

When you're organized functionally, that means your team members do the exact same or similar job as you, and your direct peers all work in a similar problem domain (**FIG 5.2**). Your manager has expertise in your field, and your area leader will understand more deeply the challenges you face.

One big drawback here is that "us versus them" thinking can erupt between departments. You may start to hear some blame-filled language: "We're selling everything, and marketing does nothing," for example. If you're a global company, you'll see some culture clash here, because the engineer from Germany will have different expectations than the vice president of engineering from California. Sometimes a layer of management gets added to translate between departments; sometimes it's project or product managers who coordinate and play referee.

Alternatively, your company may have a divisional structure, which means you're organized around a particular line of business, region, or market (**FIG 5.3**). Larger companies with offices in multiple regions may be structured by global region. The benefits here include efficient communication—you'll get an answer to your question faster, and in terms you understand—and you're probably closer to the customer you serve. You can learn from those in adjacent domains and get a fuller understanding of how the company brings a product to market.

However, your area leader may not have expertise in your domain, which means you'll need to sell your ideas in a way

FIG 5.3: Organizations structured by region have cross-functional teams focused on a particular market or customer.

they understand. You may have fewer experts around who can mentor you in your area of expertise. And, at the company level, you've got duplication of roles—someone is doing the job in APAC (Asia-Pacific), and someone else is doing the same job in EMEA (Europe, the Middle East, and Africa). Also, "mini cultures" are bound to pop up, both because of the culture of the physical location (Brazil is different than San Francisco) and because regions have different leaders.

These two structures aren't in opposition to each other, and many companies find some blend that works for them. A common pattern is to have a centralized marketing department, but structure sales by region. Another is formally grouping teams by function, but then also informally by project (also referred to as a matrix).

As the organizational chart firms up, you can draw inferences about how leadership wants the company to run. You'll see clues in the lines of communication that form (standup meetings, monthly business review, all-hands) as ways leaders want to align departments, address misunderstandings, and mitigate conflict.

In the words of Silicon Valley veteran and former Stripe COO Claire Hughes Johnson:

Yeah, I think a problem I've seen is people think there's going to be this perfect system and process that's going to not have any flaws, and they're always like, "Oh, it's not perfect. We got to optimize it further." And what I find is it's always just like, this is the best one you can come up with at the time. This is the best idea you have now. There's going to be flaws. Just work around those flaws. But just know there's never going to be the one thing that works. [...] There's no perfect org structure, there's no perfect operating approach, there's no perfect, yeah, performance and management and level system. But having one and committing to it is good. And don't let the perfect be the enemy of the good. (https://bkaprt.com/scw48/05-03)

In the world of high-growth organizations, almost every structure is temporary. Analyze what works well in your current structure and apply it to accomplishing your goals. If you're grouped with marketing, collaborate with them to get your ideas out there. If you're working with a leader outside your domain, find something to appreciate about them, or something they can teach you.

You may also find that this is too much structure for you, and you prefer larger, more ambiguous roles. I remember when this happened to me—the company formalized a product function, and they built out their hiring processes. I was reading a sample job description that clearly articulated what the company expected from a product owner. While that formality and detail would probably come across as professional to someone who enjoys structure, my whole body cried, "Check, please!" If this sounds like you, we'll dig more into role formalization in the next chapter.

Market demands at odds with mission

This one is a real bruiser. As your company grows to support larger and larger customers, the demands of those customers can and do contradict the company's original mission. How a company weathers these decisions can be a tea-leaf reading for employees. If you've worked at a startup, you can probably think of a flash point, a decision that walked back on the mission. For employees in Big Tech, that might be Facebook's response to election tampering (https://bkaprt.com/scw48/05-04, subscription required); or, to go old-school, Google's bowing to Chinese censorship (https://bkaprt.com/scw48/05-05).

Fortune 500 companies, or even just public companies, have fiduciary pressure for growth that can drive ethically murky— or straight-up wrong—decisions.

If the company's founders are still around, a balance between mission and market demands is more likely. But when the organization jumps from product / market fit to hypergrowth, these sorts of questions come up, and that makes for a Big Inflection Point.

Though you can usually feel the erosion of the mission through customer demands, you can also see it in product direction. Sometimes the need for efficiency overwrites the company's original vision. Maybe now you're serving a customer you don't particularly care for. Dana Lawson, senior vice president of engineering at Netlify, described to me how that drift can play out:

> *Around the hypergrowth stage, that's when you start dealing with the heartbreak around attachment to the mission. You gotta grow up, and with that comes more bureaucracy, keeping your costs under control, differentiating your product in the market. That's when you start looking at other products and building features directly to compete, in order to neutralize the market. You're shipping pricing and packaging changes, not the original serotonin itch from your early days. And I'm dealing with that heartbreak right now, with a staff engineer who was an early hire, she thinks we're too corporate.*

If you came to the role thinking you were going to democratize widgets, and now you're building widgets for the enterprise, that's a big shift. Let's take your temperature about it:

- From 1 (not at all) to 5 (totally), how would you rate the company's current alignment with the original mission?
- From 1 (not at all) to 5 (totally), how does the company align with your Possible Future right now?

EXPECTATIONS RESET: WHEN "GOOD ENOUGH" IS NO LONGER GOOD ENOUGH

Tech has quite the collection of maxims—you've likely heard these phrases repeated in meetings, conference talks, and think-pieces:

Don't let the perfect be the enemy of the good. If you're not embarrassed by the first version of your product, you've launched too late. Go from zero to one. Your product needs to crawl before it can walk, and walk before it can run.

One cliché about the tech industry is that it values speed over quality. Get the thing out the door as fast as possible. Ship it and call it a day.

But around the hypergrowth phase, those priorities flip. Quality will rival and often trump speed. Does the organization still want quick growth? Of course. But the expectations are higher. "Quick and dirty," "bubblegum and duct tape," "hacks," and "makeshift" are no longer acceptable rallying cries. Lawson shared with me how success brings with it more pressure and higher expectations:

> When you're small you can afford to be a little sloppy, when you're in that "big vision, get things done" mode. But as soon as you are a "key tool" that other developers' workflows depend on, the expectation for quality goes up. Way up. Key tools don't go down. At the same time, you have more tech debt than you've ever had before.

Although Lawson was referring to the demands on engineering in particular, every department starts to expect excellence, especially customer-facing functions. Users will expect a response to their support request within the hour. Marketing emails need to be on brand—no more Mailchimp watermark—and free of typos.

No matter your department or your function, you will likely feel the pressure of raised expectations:

- **Process.** You're not inventing, you're optimizing.

- **Behavior.** You're not saving the day; you're sustaining the product.
- **Output.** You'll be measured against plans and goals, not tickets.

Process designed around repetition

Once you've found product / market fit, you'll have to replicate dozens of business activities as you scale. Whether it's a process for sales contracts, a process for first-party event design, or vendor onboarding, this is a phase where leaders detect patterns and set up teams to perform repeatable tasks more efficiently.

Here's a sample of the processes that each department will implement to scale their operations (**FIG 5.4**). Instead of figuring it out as you go, or YOLO'ing every new problem, your department will put together a process and expect you to follow it.

Benchmarking

The demands of scale shine a light on processes that take too much time, or involve too many people. But to improve that process, first you'll need to measure it. To move more contracts through legal, you need to know how long each contract review takes. To move more leads through the funnel, you need to know your current throughput.

At this point, you might not have any reliable data. So teams must allocate time and capital to "benchmarking" activities. I remember the weeks it took to get ours in a data warehouse, and then the time it took to write solid queries we could rely on. It was months before we had working dashboards. But once we did, that dashboard became front-and-center important.

Benchmarking activities can rub early hires the wrong way. They might hate feeling watched, or that the data capture will slow their roll. Expect some pushback, defensiveness, and general "get off my lawn" gruffness from early employees who think they have some special sauce.

DEPARTMENT	EXAMPLE THAT SPECIALIZED EXPERTS WILL IMPLEMENT
Product	Release process Objectives and key results Changelog
Sales	CRM implementation Deal desk approvals
Finance	Head count approval Monthly business review Procurement Accounts payable
Marketing	Customer funnel metrics Campaign logistics Lead conversion tracking
Human Resources	Leveling Performance evaluations Candidate tracking / recruiting software
Engineering	Sprint planning Team-level code review Security review

FIG 5.4: Processes that change culture: here is a smattering of the processes you'll see as part of an organization's growth phase. More "together" organizations may have these earlier.

Following standard operating procedures

Efficiency can also mean following an established path rather than constantly inventing something new. For training teams, that means following the curriculum every time. For product teams, it means following the release process to the letter instead of launching whenever you want. If you put autonomy at the top of your "must-have" list, this phase can be tough. You're paving the way for a consistent, standardized process.

Emergence of data-driven decision-making

As decision-making shifts from intuitive—often rooted in one individual's vision—to data-driven, it can feel threatening to someone whose opinion was the sole voice of truth. Lynn Wallenstein, senior vice president of engineering at CargoSense, told me that the shift from relying on an individual's own expertise to a shared understanding was particularly tough:

> *People who are there early lean a lot on instinct—they are making the product up as they go along. I'm going to prioritize what I think is important. And then all of a sudden you move to a cycle of being customer-driven. Folks who were there early, they struggle with that prioritization: Should I follow my own instincts, or should I become a feature factory, where I work on small bugs but not on the big vision sort of work you used to do? And then at scale, you're spending time writing playbooks, and doing things that make it easier for folks who are earlier in their careers. If you've done this cycle multiple times, it feels natural.*

As mechanisms pop up to ensure that the company maintains a level of quality, more eyes will be on your work. You'll need to persuade and get approvals. In other words, there's more process, which can make early employees particularly grumpy. Mary Moore-Simmons, vice president of engineering at AgentSync, described to me how early employees struggle to let go of the ego involved in their work:

> *They're unhappy because they used to make all the decisions themselves. They never had to convince anyone of anything. But our product is larger now, we have teams of ten people that are working on different parts of the product, and you can't just go off in a corner and do whatever you want. You have to talk to your team, get buy-in, and agree to a solution together.*

As the organization matures, the activities that make you successful in that role will shift—even if you have the same title. The organization wants fewer heroics and a more holistic approach to projects—one that considers the wider company's needs.

What got you a bonus can now get you fired

I remember the rush of getting paged late at night, when the application would go down, the magic of coming together against this imminent threat, and the epic victory once we conquered the problem. The app needs you, it can't survive without you, you are its only hope.

That whole process is unsustainable. It's about ego, not about the application's health. These kinds of heroic habits—being paged on a weekend, fixing a bug for a big customer—can be hard to break, because they make you feel important. But as the team grows, that concentration of knowledge is a liability for the company, and hoarding knowledge will earn you poor performance reviews. Moore-Simmons went on to draw a bright line:

> Engineers who report to me don't always understand that if they are the sole person that owns something, and it's not documented, they're in my crosshairs. Their job is not more secure. It is less secure.

Wallenstein told me that this moving target for what's considered "good" behavior is hard, and it frustrates early-stage employees:

> Particularly for folks who have been there for a while, that's hard to reconcile: "Hey, I did the same thing two years ago, and you gave me a big bonus—what gives?" Employees need to understand where the company is at in its life cycle. There's a difference between staying up until 4:00 a.m. and pushing code to master, force-deploying and saving the day, and then three years later having security breathing down your neck.

Early notions of "good" often rest within one person's area of genius and getting urgent tasks done by brute force. Later notions of "good" include more people, alignment, and planning. This is the shift from reactive work to proactive work.

The shift from reactive to proactive

Early-stage companies basically run on the adrenaline hits from each completely new, totally thorny problem. It can become, in its way, an addiction—I grew to expect that pace and that pressure. When it came time to sit through eight hours of planning meetings, focusing on resource allocation or department review, doing those things never felt like actually *working*. Now, that's problematic (for personal and professional reasons), but the takeaway here is that, as an organization matures, the expectations around time and progress change.

Planning, like good design, requires time—you can feel whether a product or experience is slapdash or intentional. In the hypergrowth phase, ironically, the addition of process slows down the pace of shipping, because of the speed bumps put in place to ensure only excellent product gets to see daylight. Maybe it's a weekly product meeting, where each area demos their progress; shows how they are using data to make choices; and integrates what the competition is doing. Maybe it's even more outward-looking, and the organization is doing head-count planning for the year.

Chris McDermott, currently vice president of engineering at Wallaroo, reflected on his time with SendGrid during this sort of shift. He shared with me that he framed planning as a series of shared commitments that added up to an understanding of his team's capacity:

Initially, we didn't plan, we didn't make commitments or anything. We operated on tickets, a day-to-day and week-to-week thing. When we first tried to get all of the engineering teams and the product managers to plan a quarter's worth of work, that was a big deal. Nobody had ever done that before. Product matured when we got a new chief product officer, which changed how we prioritized things, and how we reported on status.

Business planning (and its beloved twin, business reporting) means that the company is investing time and capital in deliberating about what's next. Whether it's six-page proposal documents like at Amazon, sprint planning like at SendGrid, or objectives and key results, these mechanisms embody the organization's future strategy. The tools your team previously used to reflect your progress may have been pretty "bottom up"—*ad hoc* lists, team-specific kanbans, Trello boards. Once your company has shifted to a forward-looking, strategic place, management will want to see the whole organization's progress, at a very high level.

And here's where enterprise software enters the chat.

YOUR TOOLSET IS YOUR CULTURE

Think about your first day on the job. How many applications did you need to create credentials for? Email, chat, the product itself, and maybe, maaaaaybe a wiki. Do you use different tooling now? Probably.

The homegrown tools that got you to a hundred people require too much precious dev time to maintain. As organizations grow, they standardize tools across teams to open up capacity, streamline their operations, and enable faster onboarding. You've got increased security concerns. You've got a grown-up customer relationship manager to track sales.

In 2000, Joel Spolsky's "The Joel Test" suggested twelve metrics for assessing the quality of a developer team (https://bkaprt.com/scw48/05-06). It's hard to imagine now, but coming out of an era of "code monkeys," technologists clamored for management to respect their profession. The ninth item asked: "Do you have the best tools money can buy?"

Twenty-some years later, I'd posit: Who decides what's "best"? Employees or management? When the choice is out of the team's hands, that's a breaking point for many early employees. During a conversation I had with Mary Moore-Simmons, she reflected on respecting engineers and their preferred workflow:

The moment I decided to quit was a little less than a year before I did. We needed to pick a monitoring software. Microsoft has a homegrown monitoring and metrics collection software, and the engineers hated using it. I figured out solutions they were happy with, and sent a proposal document to our VP. He told us no: not only were we forced to use the Microsoft tools, we were also going to be forced to migrate all our existing software to tools that engineering hated. And I thought, "I'm quitting!"

In in their book *Accelerate: The Science of Lean Software and DevOps*, Nicole Forsgren, Jez Humble, and Gene Kim point out that even in the enterprise, it's a best practice to allow those who do the work to select their own tooling:

Our analysis shows that tool choice is an important piece of technical work. When teams can decide which tools they use, it contributes to software delivery performance and, in turn, to organizational performance. [...] Similar results have been found in other studies of technical professionals (e.g., Forsgren et l. 2016), suggesting that the upsides of delegating tool choice to teams may outweigh the disadvantages. (https://bkaprt. com/scw48/05-07)

Individual contributors hold expertise in their domain, and it's a sign of respect to let them choose their own tools. However, that autonomy usually gets replaced by the business demands for productivity, with velocity monitoring and top-level insights.

Look at your team's current toolset and ask yourself:

- Are the tools emergent, meaning you, as an individual, can control the input? Or are they top-down, made for managers to have high-level insights?
- What do the tools optimize for?
- Do they align with or are they at odds with your Possible Future?

Your toolset reflects the organization's culture *as it stands now*. Your tools bespeak autonomy and identity: if that identity clashes with your Possible Future, you're not aligned.

THE END OF INFORMATION CHAOS

When new employees used to onboard at GitHub, we joked that you were "drinking from the firehose." All the repositories you watched sent you *all* of the notifications by default. The information was there, "transparently," but there was too much of it. A skill every Hubber had to hone was the ability to sift signal from noise, and infer where to spend their attention.

While the finer points are specific to GitHub, the experience of being overwhelmed by information is pretty common. "Information chaos" is a hallmark of early-stage and product / market fit organizations.

On a small team, there's this sense of ambient understanding. We know the leader as a person, individually, and what they're about. As the team expands, that becomes a challenge. Information becomes staggered or given out on a need-to-know basis. You may notice the creation of a corporate communications department, and blog posts begin to sound like they've been written by attorneys. Yes, the way information moves has shifted.

Transparency in tension with clarity

Many founders start a company with a certain kind of organization in mind. "We're going to be different from the megacorps on the Fortune 500. Transparent! Open! Flat org charts!" If you've ever worked in a concrete office park, with nowhere to walk but in circles around a sad pond surrounded by mean geese—a very particular kind of corporate hell—you may find this fresh approach to work appealing.

The leaders make themselves accessible and the best ones feel authentic. All-hands meetings may have anonymous questions that anyone can ask the leadership team. Leaders may present key metrics or results openly, and share their analysis of the data.

When you can walk up to an executive and speak to them directly, you get immediate feedback. Do they know the projects you're working on? What's their expression and first response to your question? From these informal chats it's easy to see that they are human and imperfect, and you can get a sense of who they are. Former GitHub COO Erica Brescia, who cofounded the software company Bitnami, described this implicit trust as a period of organizational grace:

When you are small, around fifty people, everyone knows the founder pretty well. If you do something stupid, they know your intentions are good. After fifty people it's hard to have that implicit trust, those personal connections with everyone on the team.

Brescia names the shift in terms of company size, and I'd add the depth of the organizational chart. With every layer that you're removed from the leader, it becomes harder to give them the benefit of the doubt. That change usually coincides with a need to have a consistent message, so that leaders don't confuse people, and send the same signal in every direction. In her conversation with me, Brescia continued:

This shift triggers a need to have a consistent communications plan for big changes. When you're a small team of five or ten people, operating with a lot of ambiguity is fine. But you get to a phase, it feels like when you get to fifty-ish people, it makes sense to be more thoughtful about what is communicated and when.

Planning how you're going to communicate and when is so important—employees expect you to have answers, consider edge cases, and know the implications of your decisions. There's tension around timing, and around trust: the company needs to be intentional about their message at a time when growth means that access to the leader may have diminished. As an employee, you'll see this happen in rifts where early-stage employees build bridges of understanding to the founders, while later employees default to suspicion.

Clarity in tension with legality

In the hypergrowth phase, the sensitivity of information increases by orders of magnitude. News about product, customers, or layoffs can signal an IPO or destabilize a potential acquisition deal. You're limited to what you can say, especially with regard to nonpublic information. As a result, leaders can't be as clear or transparent as they used to be.

Graham Neray, CEO of Oso and formerly chief of staff at MongoDB, told me there were two areas where they needed to reboot their communications: information from board meetings (since it was confidential), and conversations with new hires about equity:

> *How we talked about equity had to change. We couldn't draw conclusions for the candidate about how the stock would perform—we could point to market data, and they could make their own inferences from that. You want to discuss it in a way that is attractive to the candidate, try to show them there will be upside for them, but also credible and within the lines of what you're legally allowed to do.*

It's easy to imagine how these restrictions can make for a conversational game of Twister for everyone involved. Some leaders leave their answers open and vague, and sometimes that's the right call.

As an employee, once you begin to see legalese creep into everyday speech, you've passed an authenticity threshold; leaders you admire may no longer sound like the accessible, real humans you used to work closely with. The reason why may be worth knowing to you, or it might not. Questions to ask yourself:

- Is your comfort zone early-stage "good enough" or later-stage "excellence"?
- Can you accept and integrate the change in expectations for your role?
- Does your current toolset let you to do your best work?
- What patterns do you see in the way information flows through the organization?

ORDER WILL EMERGE FROM THE MAYHEM

Santiago's quote earlier in this chapter about "breaking culture" is harsh because the company can indeed feel broken. Nothing works the way it used to, or quite as well as it should.

We can think of this painful, messy breaking process as molting. The company's next iteration will have a harder shell, in the form of more structure. Let's take a look at the systems and structures that consistently emerge as the organization reaches the hypergrowth phase.

6 STRUCTURES AND SYSTEMS

WHEN I FIRST JOINED GITHUB, I'd put my work-related expenses on my personal AmEx. I saw this as a win-win—our group made decisions quickly, and the rewards points were an added bonus.

After the acquisition, it was a different story—everything over a certain dollar amount needed to go through a complex, multistep process, where finance approved the budget, legal approved the contract, and security approved the software. Then everything matched up with a purchase order (that had its own separate routing).

Spending the budget (funds I had *already* lobbied to get for the team) felt like a second job. I struggled for the approvals of stakeholders who didn't understand our activities. Procurement was, admittedly, an underresourced function, and new to the organization. One day, I found myself bumping up against a deadline. Remembering the ease of only six months ago, I decided to put a charge on my personal AmEx card and call it a day.

That was a mistake.

When Enron's shady accounting practices leveled the energy industry and took a big chunk of value of the stock market with them, Congress clapped back with a new set of accounting and bookkeeping practices to prevent bad actors from hiding cobwebs in their books. Publicly traded companies have to show where the money goes, put up big contracts for a public bidding progress, and generally show a paper trail for accountability's sake. That group of regulations is called the Sarbanes-Oxley Act, and it's no joke. Not only did my hand get slapped, in public, by a head of finance, but I had to go back and do all the work anyway.

Until that moment, I hadn't seen the organization as having to comply with the demands of a wider system: a *federal* system of financial accountability. We were on a different playground entirely—one with firm expectations for how funds should be allocated, documented, and tracked.

You've felt the shock waves that indicated the culture was breaking as it wrestled with new challenges. Now it's time to look at what the culture is becoming (**FIG 6.1**). Structures and systems arise as the company lays the groundwork for an IPO or acquisition, specifically around these areas:

- **Finance:** In the hypergrowth phase, the organization needs to meet financial goalposts. It will expect line managers (and individual contributors!) to know the return on investment of their team, and use basic accounting practices.
- **Team structure:** Get ready for the organizational design to formalize, with a "translation layer" of management.
- **Scope of role:** New expectations about your role will come down the pike, measured more precisely, and with a narrower scope.

Whether you consider these new systems a structure to fight against or a support system to relax into depends on your point of view. You can make hay out of the opportunities that arise as the structure takes shape. Let's dig into what to expect, and how to make the most of the changes.

Alignment: an ongoing dialogue

You |—————————————— — ——————————————| The company

Accept and integrate

Changes in the organization

You are here

Articulating what you want

Company sets goals

Finding alignment

Discovering what you want

New challenges

FIG 6.1: The company will set goals needed to successfully "exit," and will introduce structures and systems to guide the organization as it matures.

ACCOUNTING, BEING ACCOUNTED FOR, AND BEING ACCOUNTABLE

The humbling example of my foibles with federal accounting regulations aside, if you want to get anything done past the product / market fit phase, the finance department is your friend. This function will expand as you grow, perhaps most radically in head count and depth of expertise. Managers can expect to present business cases and attach their activities to a cost center to track their spend.

For those of you who are individual contributors, that means your team will need to show a concrete return on investment. Say you're feeling really squeezed, so you ask your manager for additional team members (or "head count"). Each additional "head" will need to correspond to specific results, whether they concern engagement, revenue, compliance, or the related goal for your team. You can support your manager's business case for expanding your team by coming to them *with data*.

For line managers, the introduction of cost centers and profit centers means you're going to be accountable for your "spend," a.k.a. your investment. What will you have to show for it? You may not know how to do this. That's okay—good leaders help you learn on the job. This is all to say that while I'm not an expert in finance, here are the bits that ended up mattering when I took my book learning to work.

A quick business primer

For high-growth organizations, there are three outcomes. The company will:

1. go public,
2. get acquired, or
3. fail.

So when the company has validated demand (product / market fit), the next goalpost is planning for the first or second scenarios.

You'll see the organization take steps to get its financial house in order. Common metrics around marketing effectiveness, like customer lifetime value, customer acquisition cost, and retention rate will enter the conversation. Even the research and development side of the house will feel the influence of financial metrics.

When you peek at companies that are already public, you can see how these metrics eventually add up to how the company gets evaluated, at the highest level. That's worth paying attention to, because the company's valuation—how much the whole enchilada is worth—derives from ratios involving these numbers.

If you're anything like this aging millennial who grew up reading the panel of their cereal box, you're familiar with the math: for every cup of cereal, here are the vitamins and minerals you get. Financial statements are like the nutritional information for the entire box. For example, inside a box of Airbnb in 2023 is almost $8.5 billion in revenue (**FIG 6.2**).

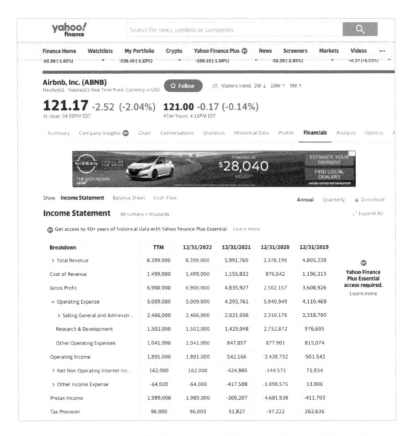

FIG 6.2: Financial statements of public companies, like this one for Airbnb from Yahoo Finance, show all the important metrics for company valuations (https://bkaprt.com/scw48/06-01).

Depending on the stage of your company, the organization might put an emphasis on different line items. Two line items will be important for you, strategically, in framing your ideas and understanding a company's order of operations: Cost of Goods Sold, and General, Selling, and Administrative expenses.

Cost of Goods Sold

You might hear about *Cost of Goods Sold* (COGS) and improving the *margin*, or rate of profit, for their initiatives. Dana Lawson elaborated on this during one of our conversations:

> *At that Series D stage, there are more expectations around fiscal responsibility, you want to be in good shape when the company gets acquired or goes public. You gotta keep that contribution margin around 20 percent, keep your cost of goods sold under control.*

COGS is the money spent to make the product. When you're early-stage, the focus is on making the thing and finding out if selling the thing will be profitable. This is one of the reasons early investment focuses on the research and development side of the house.

R & D functions roll up into the COGS category, which the business can "write off" on their taxes. The US government also has tasty tax credits to incentivize spend in this area. COGS costs per unit ideally go down as you reach economies of scale.

Since the business model is getting hammered out (a.k.a. "iterated upon"), you probably won't invest too much in growth or go-to-market initiatives just yet. The business would be in danger of growing too fast too quickly.

You might hear folks talk about getting the "pacing" of the company's growth right. Invest in sales or marketing too early, and the company might have to walk back commitments they've made to customers when you change direction. The wrong pace can also result in layoffs when the company needs to go back to the drawing board with its business model.

General, Selling and Administrative

General, Selling, and Administrative (G&A) is an operating expense (often referred to as "OpEx") that includes your sales reps, your growth hackers, your product marketers. The company activates these folks *after* product / market fit. Why?

Because *first* the organization has to find people to care about the product, and *then* figure out how to package it in a way that scales. Leaders constantly balance the pressure to grow at breakneck speed with making sure their business is in good financial health.

If your role falls under G&A, that funding can wax and wane due to macro trends (like recession) and it doesn't enjoy the same tax incentives. Ergo, these roles tend to be vulnerable to layoffs. It's always helpful to track your ROI (as we did in Chapter 1), but it's especially important for these roles.

THE IMPACT OF SPECIALIZATION

In the early days of an organization, everyone is a unique snowflake with their own special blend of talents, and your organization is probably pretty flat. Everyone tends to cover more than one area of expertise. You might have an engineering lead who gives great conference presentations, or a marketer who has a background in systems design.

Since everyone's background is a unique mélange of flavors, when you hire additional people, you're looking to fill gaps. This is definitely the way I've thought about candidates and their talents—do we have that capability on the team already? How will their knowledge of one area complement what we already do? Do they have the expertise we need to expand into a new area? It's all about designing a flexible, high-performing squad, and at smaller sizes, each individual hire and their rapport with the team really matters.

In the hypergrowth phase, you need to replicate that success—faster, at a higher level of quality, and you also have to manage risk. So instead of having a multifaceted generalist who "kind of" grooms the backlog when they have time, the company decides: *If we're going to do product-led growth, we should have a formal product organization. And now that we have a product organization, we need to hire the best product managers.*

Pretty soon you'll see more people with the same title and the same common job description. New hires previously held a similar position at another company. The same thing happens

Early-stage	Product / market fit	Hypergrowth
• Everyone does everything	• Functions formed • Hires with specialized expertise	• Strong general domain knowledge, laser focus

FIG 6.3: A role's scope changes as the organization matures.

in sales (with geographical coverage being a common organizational principle), marketing, engineering, support, and so on.

Your team-wide meetings have gotten larger, and during video conference meetings, it's possible people don't even turn their cameras on anymore—in a sea of thumbnails, your face won't be missed. Because your business unit now contains so many subteams, only so much of this overview conversation will be relevant to you. You're focused on a specific business process, or a slice of the product, or piece of the infrastructure. With the emergence of functions (or departments) and experts, the role's size and scope has narrowed in focus (FIG 6.3).

In the hypergrowth phase, there's a standard model for your role at the company. At this point, you have clear expectations of what you should be working on and what success looks like. This shift has implications for decision-making, the expected scope of your role (or any role), and the communication "swimlanes" of the organization.

Managers: a layer to coordinate and translate between specialties

Many founders just love making things. They didn't start their business in order to *hire managers*. Some are uncomfortable with traditional notions of power and don't want to perpetuate it. A good chunk of them hate red tape and bureaucracy, and want to "hire brilliant people and get out of the way."

But one day they realize they need to build out a function they don't really understand very well. Let's say it's something specialized, like security. They don't know how to assess the expertise of a junior person, they don't know how to teach, or how to lead in this domain to train that person. And yet they need them to be operational from day one. They need an expert—so they hire a leader.

Now this security leader's job is to take the business goals, which are likely still in founder-speak, and connect the day-to-day security work toward those goals. This new leader can gauge the skill level of candidates, level up junior staffers, and break down vague directions into items that security specialists can act on and see as valuable.

Hierarchy is a tool to connect with the wider organization, and it clarifies the team's focus—a focus that has the potential to change with shifting business goals.

Where business goals go, team structures follow

Imagine you're the CEO, and you have a set of goals you want to accomplish that are different from last year's because the market has changed. The competition has introduced a new feature, or there's a chip shortage, or new security threats leave your application vulnerable. You have a thousand engineers at your disposal. Do you see them as individual teams, with their own special powers, interests, and pet projects? Or do you see them as a collective might that you can rally to solve a Big Business Problem?

The idea behind this reframing is to help you see why there's so much change among teams. Stop thinking about your individual role for a moment, and think about your department as a "capability" that (hopefully) gets stronger as you add more expertise to the mix. Strategically oriented leaders see the organization in terms of dedicating investment to achieve specific outcomes. Strategy is where the resources go for maximum impact. Teams form around business goals, and if those change, they need to quickly adapt to be able to focus on something else.

Within departments, managers will frequently form and dissolve teams to make sure they effectively distribute the brain power and expertise of individual contributors. Lynn Wallenstein told me she refers to this as seniority "load balancing" when she's forming teams around Objectives and Key Results.

We used a concept of a squad, which might have one to two staff engineers, two senior engineers, maybe four eng 2s or engs 3s, maybe a junior if your team wasn't brand new. If your squad has nine principals, that is not going to work.

This can be very hard for those early employees who don't see their skills as interchangeable. Especially if you're a subject matter expert, or if you're really motivated by a mission for a particular product or initiative, take heed of the expectation of fungibility.

What specialization and structure mean for you

The demands of the hypergrowth phase usually bring about specialization, which carries with it a layer of hierarchy. At the same time, teams come together and dissolve based on business goals and expertise. For your own role and future:

- Look around at the next step the company is going to become—the competitors, or changes that will happen. Do you prefer a larger, more ambiguous role with more autonomy, or a specialized role where you can work in your area of genius?
- If you're an individual contributor, remember your Possible Future: do you need to have management experience? This is a time where you might give it a shot. The stakes aren't that high, and you can always go back to your area of expertise.
- As functions begin to take shape and haven't become rigid yet, make your case to lead a team or a department. Whom do you need to book a meeting to make your intentions clear? How can you get on their calendar?

Another byproduct of all this specialization is a way to measure expertise, a.k.a. career levels. Let's take a look at how those usually come about, and how you can navigate the "career calibration" process.

Career ladders and leveling

At some point during the product / market fit phase, your first human resources hire probably suggested that the company roll out some career ladders. I'm not great with categories and rules but I've come around on career ladders, and have even developed them for a cross-functional team. Like finance and management, there's a fair amount of jargon here you should know, so let's spell some of these concepts out:

- *Career ladders* are established pathways for each function in an organization, from entry-level to most senior.
- *Levels* are the individual rungs on that career ladder, with clear expectations for skill and area of impact.
- Your job title may correspond to your level. You may hear engineers refer to themselves by level, like "E5" or "E3."
- The process of calibrating or assessing roles to see where they fall on the ladder is commonly referred to as *leveling*.
- Each level has corresponding *salary bands*, a term that refers to a range of compensation, depending on the role's value to the organization, and your geographic location if you're remote. It's possible to get a raise within your band without getting a promotion in level.

Larger technology companies always have a range of career ladders and levels (**FIG 6.4**). During the product / market-fit phase, you may not have them at all, or you will have far fewer of them.

Levels and company maturity

Most early-stage organizations don't have levels. Everyone is doing a little of everything. During the product / market-fit phase, the system will be lightweight, with maybe one to three levels of junior, midlevel, and expert. During hypergrowth, when you have more specialized teams, you'll start to see longer ladders, with more levels (**FIG 6.5**). Deva Santiago told me that a company's leveling philosophy will change over its life cycle:

× Facebook	× Microsoft	× Google	× Standard
	SDE		
	59	L3	Entry Level Engineer
E3	60	SWE II	New Grad
	SDE II		
	61	L4	Software Engineer
E4	62	SWE III	
	Senior SDE		
	63	L5	Senior Engineer
E5	64	Senior SWE	
	Principal SDE		
	65	L6	Staff Engineer
E6	66	Staff SWE	Senior Staff Engineer
	67	L7	
E7	Partner	Senior Staff SWE	Principal Engineer
	68	L8	
E8	69	Principal Engineer	Distinguished Engineer
	70	L9	Fellow
E9	Distinguished Engineer	Distinguished Engineer	
	80	L10	
	Technical Fellow	Google Fellow	

FIG 6.4: Levels.fyi is a great resource for understanding levels and ladders in the tech sector. You can see how mature tech organizations use them, and how many levels there are (https://bkaprt.com/scw48/06-02).

I usually start with five or six levels, but certain companies want to start with three and that's fine. What's important is that you map it to market data. Your compensation bands may be wider if you only have three, and there's a lot more crossover between 1 and 2, and 2 and 3. So it's important for employees to understand that leaders are mapping out growth strategy, their philosophy. And they probably have different philosophies at different phases.

Lawson told me that as the organization grows, so will the number of rungs on those career ladders:

Leveling needs to be about merit, impact, and results. The more mature the organization is, there needs to be more depth in those levels. Not moving the yardstick that it takes to progress, but because you're a more established organization, there's more complexity there.

Early-stage
- No levels, loose titles

Product / market fit
- 1-3 basic levels
- Performance reviews

Hypergrowth
- Career ladders and progression
- Compensation bands
- Geography-based pay

FIG 6.5: The development of career ladders and depth of leveling systems vary at different organizational stages.

For startups, leveling systems are *dynamic*. If you stay at an organization for four years—the common duration for stock option cliffs—you'll be leveled more than once. That means you should be prepared to have your skills assessed, and to have your role's ROI handy.

Similar to when you're designing systems, when you focus on one goal, it's at the expense of another. Maybe you're optimizing for speed at the expense of quality. Or you're sacrificing depth for scale. The same is true about career levels and ladders—there are no perfect systems, just ones that have prioritized choices in their design.

Values-based systems

Even if you can't name a company's values off the top of your head, you can describe its vibes—how the product feels, how decisions get made, what the copy in your employee handbook sounds like. When values are done right, they touch all aspects of the organization, including the design of your ladders and levels. When I spoke with Erica Brescia, she pointed to Bitnami's values as a driver of culture, and also a criteria of evaluation:

> *If I go back to Bitnami, our values were quite clear and clearly embedded in how we operated, from performance reviews to the feedback we gave. It created a very powerful culture. It wasn't wildly creative, but we had five core values—empower*

users, stay curious, team up, make it so, value simplicity. We'd
evaluate candidates on the values, and incorporated those
values into performance reviews.

Other companies may value traits like transparency and openness. One tech company I'm aware of is so committed to that value that any employee can see their progression in the career ladder at any time *and can add their own data*. When they meet more than 50 percent of the criteria for a more advanced role, that action automatically triggers their manager and HR for a promotion discussion.

Others may value personal growth, and that translates into their levels and evaluation design.

Drawing a clear path

More established organizations have the benefit of a learning trajectory, so you know what to focus on. Santiago highlighted this aspect of the levels to me as well: "Levels also create the opportunity to strive for the next level, whether it's 3, 8, or 15."

If you think about an organization like Microsoft, where the average tenure is north of five years (https://bkaprt.com/scw48/06-03), people are going to want to grow in their roles—they need somewhere to go, somewhere to put that motivation. And if you look at employee development at a high level, the organization's ability to learn and adapt is a competitive advantage (https://bkaprt.com/scw48/06-04, PDF).

Promoting fairness

Initially, I was drawn to Reed Hastings's *The No Rules Rules* decree that compensation bands (and the levels associated with those bands) are a waste of time and effort (https://bkaprt. com/scw48/06-05). For Hastings, these sorts of categories and assumptions are tough to square with the nature of constantly changing knowledge work. Just pay top of market and call it a day.

This approach appealed to me for several reasons. What manager doesn't want their team members to feel valued with the highest compensation? As a generalist myself, I was unconvinced that managers needed to be gatekeepers, prescribing the next step for folks in various domains. If people don't want their careers to go in a straight line, far be it from me to prescribe their next step.

In optimizing for "avoiding rules," I wasn't paying attention to the power dynamics that shut out underrepresented groups. As part of the values-driven design, Hastings put the onus on the employee to know their worth in the marketplace. That meant the most-recent market data: job offers from other companies.

Here's the thing: more interviews mean more job offers, and white job applicants get 36 percent more interviews than black applicants and 24 percent more than Latino applicants (https://bkaprt.com/scw48/06-06, subscription required). So asking employees to bring in competitive offers puts underrepresented groups at a further disadvantage: they'll get fewer offers, and need to do two to three times the work to get them.

Lawson told me that she agrees strongly that levels work toward fairness:

> *Leveling is important because of equity—it gives the opportunity for introverts, people who speak English as a second language, underrepresented folks to get gauged on merit, impact, and results. If you don't have levels, I guarantee you that power structures revert to baseline.*

When your organization rolls out its leveling system, chances are that it's going to hurt. Maybe you and your manager aren't on the same page in terms of your experience or seniority. Or the system is optimized in a way that's not aligned with your values. It doesn't feel good to be seen as a number. Unfortunately, there's a truth to that—those are the implications of "scale."

Roles get really narrow

The flip side of clarity around your role means that the scope of your role is more restricted. Chris McDermott described this process to me as a narrowing of lanes:

Before you have the career development framework, with all the titles and the levels mapped out, it's a lot squishier. Once you start to create those titles and levels, it all gets more specific. Then people have lanes, and they tend to stay in the lanes for the most part. Early on, I think those lanes are still pretty wide. But as the company grows, the lanes get narrower and narrower. By the time you get up to a couple thousand people, you're in a pretty narrow lane.

This narrowing is not necessarily the case for directors and above. My sense is that for more mature organizations, the way to move up and get promoted is to absorb more and more things under your umbrella.

But if you're an individual contributor or a line manager, you'll be assessed on a rubric that's specific to your domain, your role's core activities. So, engaging in activities outside those guidelines—like committee work, interviewing candidates, or cleaning up documentation—typically won't "count" as fulfilling your role. Everything you do should be within the scope of your role or otherwise recognized as a value-add. If you're not sure, ask your manager.

Around about this time, a big power shift occurs between you and your manager too—they become a gatekeeper to progress, or one of a team of "deciders." Expect promotions to take longer and have more people involved. Prepare to advocate for yourself. In my experience pitching promotion packets in leadership meetings, I never saw anything mean-spirited or untoward—most folks want to recognize great people. Even so, that process is a black box to an individual contributor, and it's hard to influence a result in that situation.

On the other hand, when lots of people have a similar role to yours, it creates a bit of cushion. More than one person knows how to do your job, and you won't be leaving anyone in the lurch if you need to take parental or medical leave. The expectations of you are probably the most reasonable they've been since the early days of the company. If you want to stay for the ride, you can exhale and lean into the support the structure gives you.

STRUCTURE IS ALSO SUPPORT

To some, rules can feel like a trap. But to others, rules are evidence of the company's maturity, and the processes help them have better alignment with the rest of their lives. Then there are folks somewhere in between—they sense that there are trade-offs.

Tilde Ann Thurium told me that the established processes of a later-stage company can offer the security and peace of mind that early-stage companies can't:

> *The good thing about working for a large organization with processes is that those processes can also work for you. If you need to go on a leave of absence, at a five-person startup that might be complete chaos. But at a giant company, they probably have methods for administering that. There's also a budget for learning and training, where you can get really specialized. Ultimately, working at bigger companies has been a good move for me.*

These systems aren't going away, so it's up to you figure out your relationship to them:

- Do you enjoy the structure of a more established company?
- Is it important to you to have clear expectations about your role?
- Are you interested in changing projects or teams within the company every year?

Even for individual contributors, there will come a time when the company looks to roll out new systems and turns to you for help. In the next chapter, we'll explore how to manage change.

ROLLING OUT CHANGE

Natura non facit saltum (Nature makes no leaps).
—CHARLES DARWIN, ON THE ORIGIN OF SPECIES

IF YOU'RE WITH A COMPANY for long enough, or take the plunge and decide to manage people, the company will ask you to lead a change initiative. Maybe you've been asked to:

- Integrate new tools, like project management software or a CRM
- Launch, and more importantly *support*, a new feature
- Implement new career ladders and incentives
- Bring in a new team structure or a leader

Imagine we have a colleague named Tara, a mid-level individual contributor on the People and Culture team. She was asked to roll out a change to her company's learning and development platform, with a new package of learning and development benefits. She typed up the changes, saved the document, and got on with her day. However, when some employees read the news, they were really surprised. The changes challenged their routines and expectations. They got defensive and ranted about the changes in public channels. Tara felt attacked and embarrassed. As a result, she has hesitated to speak up since then.

Sound familiar? That's probably because tech is a fast-moving environment, and no one teaches you how to adapt gracefully. An individual contributor who rolls out change poorly can damage their relationships within the organization. And a manager wants their team to be able to change nimbly—no one wants to be the next Blockbuster Video.

Grinding through miscommunication, missing the implementation of tools that could help the organization scale, ignoring damaged relationships that inhibit the ability to get things done—all contribute to the decay of an organization. That's what's at stake here.

This chapter will introduce you to a framework you can use to boost adaptability, reduce dread around change, message change clearly, and measure the impact of the changes you make to your team.

JUST ENOUGH CHANGE MANAGEMENT

Leading through change is hard—hard and lonely. You know the end state, you have a sense of what needs shifting, but inviting people into that vision takes time and will almost always cause pain.

Change management refers to the human side of organizational change, offered by top-tier consulting firms to cut costs, boost profits, or redirect the organization. That sort of approach can grind through time, feel out of sync with your values, or bring up pain from horror stories at previous companies.

Through trial and error with my own teams, consulting with dozens of respected leaders, and consulting business scholarship, I developed a framework for change management that offers team members agency and autonomy. This approach also manages risk by including team members in the implementation of the new direction. I call the sequential framework AMICUS because it makes change more friendly (**FIG 7**):

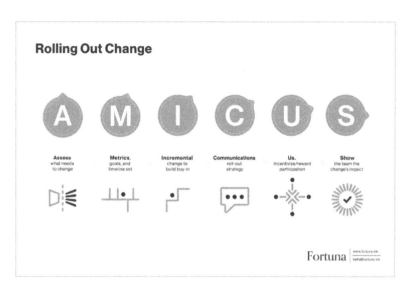

FIG 7: AMICUS is a lightweight framework for change management.

1) **A:** *Assess* what needs to change.
2) **M:** Set *metrics*, goals and a timeline.
3) **I:** Build buy-in with *incremental* change.
4) **C:** Create a *communications* plan.
5) **U:** Incentivize and reward *us* for participating in change.
6) **S:** *Show* the impact of the change.

I wish I had had a framework like with the teams I served. So much confusion and pain could have been prevented with just enough change management.

ASSESS WHAT NEEDS TO CHANGE

The first step could also be called "get the data"—both the quantitative historical data, and the qualitative background from the humans. You want to find out *exactly* what needs to change. Keep an open mind, because the data may surprise you.

Discover the context and background behind previous decisions

Before you act, *listen*. Our industry is biased toward action and rewards quick decision-making, so this doesn't need to be a massively long "discovery phase"—it can take an afternoon or a couple of days.

Tell the folks who have touched the problem that you are listening to get the bigger picture. Ask about previous decisions to find out what has been tried before. Quality assurance consultant Casey Greene told me that one of her favorite leaders did just that:

> At my last gig we brought on a head of sales, who was wonderful. He had a lot of emotional intelligence, spent a lot of time understanding the technical subtleties of the product, and honestly just spent a lot of time listening to everyone. He took the time to understand how things had been done, where the roadblocks were, what had been tried, before making changes or trying new experiments.

This is the number one complaint I hear from people who feel like change "happens" to them: they don't think that decision-makers listen.

It's a lesson I learned myself when setting quarterly goals for a product in my portfolio. I took one look at the quantitative data about activation, set an arbitrary goal, and got on with my day.

When a wonderful teammate (and also the *actual* product owner) asked me about the goal, I had the sense to stop autopilot and listen. He spent two hours with me explaining the product's flow, the congestion points that were keeping it from growing, and his ideas around automation. Those two hours paid back big dividends through the trust we built, and I knew what I was talking about when I asked for more investment to support that product.

Gather the numbers

In addition to qualitative input from humans, get quantitative data from machines. A few examples:

- If you have a hunch that revenue is down because of conversion, hunt down user activity from the first seven and fourteen days of a new user experience.
- If you have a vision for self-serve versus sales-led growth, find out how long it takes to close one customer, and get a clear picture of the customer-acquisition cost.
- If you're introducing a new process to the team, drop a survey to benchmark their knowledge, or even how they feel at this point in time, I'm a big fan of this tool because it gives you insights on data that perhaps didn't previously exist.

Give yourself some time to gather the numbers because, as we discussed in Chapter 5, it's possible that there's a black hole where the data should be. If your company has a data science team that provides insights internally, introduce yourself to them right away—that will be an important relationship.

Remember our friend Tara? Here's how the assessment phase might look for her: Tara could study changes her department has made, ones that have gone well and poorly, look over any retrospective documents, and gather data on learning and development benefit usage to find out who the "power users" are who may be particularly affected by the change.

Once you have the data benchmarked, and you know what hasn't worked in the past, then you can set measurable goals for what you need to move.

SET METRICS, GOALS, AND A TIMELINE

The metrics and goals you choose will drive the changes you make, and the timeline gets everyone on the same page. Consider these pieces the anchors of your change-management strategy.

Metrics and goals

Once you have a benchmark, set a goal: What's the variable you're moving, and by how much? What will this change move from x (your benchmark) to y (your goal)? Is it more revenue, cash in the bank, faster conversion, or shorter time to merge?

If you don't home in on the target, your call for change can sound like an authoritarian parent: "Because I said so!" If the team thinks this is an arbitrary change, they might not come with you on this journey. They're not wrong to be suspicious—according to McKinsey research:

> *[O]nly 15% of executives set detailed business targets for their reorgs, and 17% of reorgs are launched at the whim of an executive or because the leadership team believes the company needs to be shaken up—reasons that typically lead to problems. (https://bkaprt.com/scw48/07-01, subscription required)*

You don't want to "just shake things up." That's a waste of effort, time, and brain cells. You want to improve something, and assess whether the change had the desired effect.

Apart from cost, speed, and adoption, here are a few other questions to ask when considering which metrics might work for you:

- Does it make the organization more efficient? For example, implementing a proactive planning process will coordinate activities across product and engineering.
- Are there fewer negative effects as a result? One of the key DevOps Research and Assessment (DORA) metrics is time to restore service, for instance (https://bkaprt.com/scw48/07-02).
- Will it affect other downstream teams or services (e.g., number of support tickets)? If other teams or services rely on you, this is an important one.

Setting a timeline

Set a deadline for your change to be completed and schedule your retrospective up front. This is your "work back" date, and it forces you to reflect on whether the effort was a success or failure. It's also a promise you're making to the team to listen to their input.
Our friend Tara might include:

- Metrics showing benefits adoption—how many people use the thing
- Metrics around a decrease in benefits cost—making the company's spend more efficient
- Sentiment analysis—use this metric if your platform has "likes" or "plus ones" or a "thumbs down" to indicate what the audience thinks
- Setting a beta phase date for feedback, a final launch date, and a date to hold a retrospective

We'll dig deeper into other considerations to keep in mind when building out your timeline, including your communications strategy, and how you can build buy-in by rolling out change incrementally.
Once you have a sense of the metrics you're trying to move, consider the smaller changes that can help you get there.

BUILD BUY-IN WITH INCREMENTAL CHANGE

Few changes require swift, rip-the-Band-Aid-off action. Instead, incremental change is easier, has less resistance, and gives people time to get acclimated. As Mary Moore-Simmons told me, smaller, incremental change has a higher success rate and better staying power:

> *Pro tip: I highly recommend small, incremental change. It's safer because it has a smaller blast radius if it goes wrong. People can also adjust to small incremental changes better. It's*

great to call out reversible decisions and set a time frame for
when you can change them. "Let's just try it for two weeks and
see if we like it. If we don't like it, we can change it."

As you set goals and a timeline for change, think about which
pieces you can chunk out into "implementation waves" that
will build momentum to the desired end state (https://bkaprt.
com/scw48/07-03). In the product management world, we talk
about the product needing to crawl before it can walk, and walk
before it can run. What is the minimum viable change you can
build upon? What are a few "quick wins" that won't shock your
team members but will get you where the org needs to go? Use
the data to validate whether the change is working and draw
the connection between small change and the larger end state.

Tara may need to break her learning and development
changes into smaller pieces so that everyone can get used to it.
Maybe she beta tests the new platform with the benefit's power
users. Perhaps she offers a "preview" webinar session or internal blog post. If it's a significant change, maybe it's rebranding
it as something besides a "benefit."

I recommend this approach if the end state is clear and
you're able to anticipate the changes. When drastic change is
necessary—the 10 percent of cases that often due to circum-
stances outside the leader's control—your highest priorities are
getting a communications plan in place and making sure your
messaging is crystal clear.

CREATE A COMMUNICATIONS PLAN

With change, *when* and *how* you talk about what's happening
is at the heart of a successful strategy. Some folks find this the
most anxiety-producing piece of the puzzle—and indeed it can
be, especially with bad news. Let the goals and metrics support
and guide you.

Determine who needs to know first (and second, and third)

This depends on the scale of the change. If it's just your team, talk to the most affected people first. If you can, provide them with options. Choices equal power.

If the change affects more than a few people, you'll need a process to find out whom to share the knowledge with first. Be aware of the toll this takes on people "in the know"—they need to carry on as if they don't have this insider knowledge, which can strain their sense of integrity. You'll want a process that brings in the right people at the right time; it's not easy for anyone.

Erica Brescia told me she saw this firsthand as she oversaw her company Bitnami's acquisition:

> With Bitnami, when we were exploring options for the future of the business, one option was an acquisition. We weren't absolutely certain the deal was going to close, and to bring folks into that uncertainty can cause a lot of stress. When we needed to, we "read in" a number of people, which we call being "in the tent."
>
> But one leader kind of figured it out, so we tented him. And his reaction was "now this sucks because I can't tell anyone." Knowing the information can be quite a burden—everyone says they want to know, until they realize how heavy that can be.

My take is that you need to balance individual choice with clarity, and not optimize 100 percent in either direction. In my experience, telling people too early leads to a culture of fear, and team members shift into survival mode. You also run the risk of distracting the team with possibilities they have no control over. Doing change with integrity, in my book, means taking the time to think through how the changes will affect people in both common and unique scenarios.

Beta test your communications

Rolling out the change gradually, doing rounds of internal marketing with managers, helps to surface objections, see patterns in reactions, and address loose threads. Natalie Nagele, former CEO of Wildbit, recommends starting with one-on-one conversations. She told me that when she implemented a layer of managers for the first time, those conversations helped her hone the message:

> *We implemented managers slowly, which is the way I always think about meaningful change. We started with individual one-on-ones first before we made the big changes. Because when you do the big announcement, you want to have heard some of the worries and concerns already, so you can directly address them. Then by the time the internal public announcement comes out, everyone is basically aware and has voiced their concerns.*

This early feedback loop provided the chance to address murky details and unintended consequences, and to shape next steps for those affected. Lynn Wallenstein recommends having a "premortem" and listing all of the potential questions team members will ask—even the bruising ones, especially the bruising ones. Identifying both the common and unique use cases will help you clarify and hone your message, and you'll prevent future panic.

QED your message

QED stands for *quod erat demonstrandum*, or "which was to be demonstrated." It's shorthand for showing the steps behind your logic, clearly and cleanly. When it comes to messaging change, you want to connect:

- the input (or inputs), or the reason this change is coming about,
- your proposed change, and
- the intended output, which are the metrics you established.

This is different but related to the exercises we did in Chapter 3 to help you make your case internally. When selling an idea internally, you're framing the message for one or a few decision-makers to say "yes." When you're messaging change, you'll need to be more sensitive to more people, and to consider the consequences of your proposed change. Remember, change hurts!

Connecting these messaging elements helps others understand the logic behind your decision. Rick Nucci, CEO of Guru, speaks from experience that being clear about the goals behind the decision can help people make sense of the change.

Neha Batra, vice president of engineering at GitHub, told me she builds on this method:

> *When enacting change on my team, I try to communicate what led me to my decisions like a proof or a logical argument. That not only helps people understand why I made my decisions, but it also clues them into what information they can provide me to change my mind.*

Maybe you've been part of an organization that was pretty flat until it became clear that it needed more structure. When implementing a layer of managers for the first time, former Wildbit CEO Natalie Nagele spelled out the reason behind needing to add hierarchy: she couldn't simultaneously be the steward of the business her employees needed her to be, *and* support the careers of fifteen individuals:

> *So I told them, you all want to be supported, doing your best work, and valued, and you need someone who can be present. I can't do that and have fifteen one-on-ones. I wanted people to understand why we were doing this, where I was coming from. And they really trusted me, because this was for the benefit of the team.*

Natalie was QED'ing her message with the team:

- Input: supporting fifteen individuals while driving the future of the business

- Proposed change: implementing a line of managers
- Intended output: providing support for all of her team

Once people understand the cause of the problem, it opens the door for folks to get into the solution space with you. They can choose to take a step forward and commit to the next phase of the company, or decide it doesn't align with their Possible Future and part ways.

For Tara, when she is rolling out change, she'll want to QED her message:

- Input: the scale of the organization demands a more cost-effective benefit
- Proposed change: moving to an all-in-one platform
- Intended output: the company will keep the benefit, but in a sustainable way

US: INCENTIVIZE AND REWARD FOLKS FOR PARTICIPATING IN CHANGE

As you begin to move toward the implementation phase, you can prevent turnover, find alignment faster, and help everyone swim in the right direction by involving more people in the process.

If you're a leader, your job is to provide the North Star—the top-level vision or metric the company is trying to hit. Collaborate with the smart people around you to come up with the "how," or the strategic path to get there.

Ida Benedetto, a director at NOBL, a progressive change management firm, advises her clients to take a similar approach to change:

> *Cocreative processes allow the people who are closest to the work have as much agency as possible over how those shifts happen. We focus on building cohorts of employees cross-functionally, and empowering them to pick an area that needs to shift within the larger context of change. They can figure out*

the simplest possible change or intervention that will help move that change forward.

As with any other product or process, you'd form a cross-functional team, pitch ideas, get feedback from the customer (in this case, you and the other employees), and iterate to improve. You can treat company change the exact same way, except for two pieces: people need to see that you've integrated their input, and participating in change often means taking on work that's above and beyond their role.

Cocreation builds trust

In 2018, I realized my current team structure was not working—I had fifteen direct reports, including interns. They were putting out increasingly specialized work and they needed domain-specific mentorship. At the same time, we were a lean organization and head count was extremely tight; I didn't have the budget or open roles to hire dedicated managers. I tried dividing the team according to infrastructure versus outreach—the "home team" and the "away team"—but the feedback I received was clear: the new team structure was even more confusing.

So for our offsite that year, I asked each team member to create an organizational chart for our team. Each individual had to think about their own work, and how that fit in with designing a larger effective team. After sketching out an org chart privately, they shared it just with me. Then, when we all came together as a group, I formed two teams and asked one side to draw an org chart by division (the customer they serve), and the other side to draw an org chart by function (the domain they work in).

When each team presented their org chart, they had to answer the following questions about their choices:

- Where did we duplicate our efforts?
- Who makes the final decisions?
- What are the implications for scale? If we add a new market?
- Where is there a danger of siloing information?

- How close is this structure to the customer, on a scale of 1 (not) to 10 (very)?

We were able to surface the assumptions and expectations that folks had about how we currently worked. Once team members saw that each way had benefits and drawbacks, they could see what trade-offs we would need to make individually and as a team to reach our goals. That was a challenging conversation, but one of my proudest moments as a leader.

Coming out of that meeting, it was clear that in order to scale the team effectively, each function needed its own mentorship and expertise. We recruited managers internally, from other teams. That was a massive change that could have gone sideways—but because we got there together, everyone understood the reasoning behind the decision, and no one was surprised.

Rewarding team involvement

Benedetto homes in on an important reason to cocreate your change strategy with your team: they are the closest to the work, they are experts in the area, and this is an opportunity to foster agency and autonomy. Don't waste their expertise, please!

However, these opportunities—through committee work, employee resource group recommendations, or informal "culture clubs"—are in addition their day-to-day work duties. It's work, and people should be compensated for it.

So when I came across Guru's approach to incentivizing and rewarding change, it was both so simple and so excellent that I wondered: "Why isn't everybody doing this?" CEO Rick Nucci told me his goals were to integrate the diversity, equity, inclusion, and belonging (DEIB) strategy across every function, not just the People Team (their internal HR team). First, they incentivized participation with additional stock options. Second, they formalized participation with an application process and one-year terms:

We formalized the 4 DEIB pillars, folks who are interested in leading one of them apply for the position, which lasts one year, and is compensated with an additional option grant. That's our way of signaling our appreciation for their contribution, and it comes out of our values.

Other ways to incentivize and reward folks for their involvement in change initiatives could be additional vacation days, learning and development budget, or a bonus.

In Tara's case, she might consider:

- Putting together a committee that could vote on which benefits system to choose
- Asking team members to try the new benefits system, and include their feedback when she rolls it out to the company
- Increasing learning and development benefits for early feedback

SHOW THE IMPACT OF THE CHANGE

Once you've implemented the change and the process for tracking your metrics, the last step in the process is to gather as a team to see if the change achieved the desired result. As Lynn Wallenstein put it to me, this anchor point is critical in ushering in change, especially in hard times:

> *The biggest thing for me is about the measurement of change. Did we have the effect we wanted to? Was the effort successful? If the change is really hard, icky, like layoffs or cost-cutting, you need to tell people why you did that. Did we need to cut our burn rate to prevent a significant financial problem in eight months, and we now have eighteen months? It's really motivating to see that change has been fruitful.*

I would usually build this into the cadence of team offsites, which we tried to do twice a year. We'd spend the first few hours reflecting on the impact of changes we made, looking at both the quantitative and the qualitative data, and then use some of those takeaways to inform our strategic planning.

As with most retrospectives, taking a look at the data tends to be a creative jumping-off point for what you do next. Mary Moore-Simmons told me that the change almost always alters the course of the team, and gets everyone in a place to critique processes for improvements:

> I've noticed that if we do change it again, it's usually not back to the original way we were doing things. It's usually a refinement upon the first change.

Now that Tara has reached the end of her change timeline, the moment has come to show her stakeholders, peers, and perhaps the company the impact of her change. She can:

- Show how the change moved the numbers you set out in your metrics
- Request and implement feedback on what to do next
- Add her notes to a collection of "prior artifacts" that colleagues can draw from in the future

WHEN YOU CAN'T ALIGN

I hope I've succeeded in hammering home the message that you can either align and step forward with the company, or take a step back. It's your choice.

At some point, in the effort to align, you might find yourself doing some tricky contortions. You might not believe the words coming out of your own mouth, or they might feel wrong to you. When you just can't get there, it's time to admit that—and move on.

8 MOVING ON

YOU KEEP TRYING TO shoehorn the company into one that will work for you, until one day the realization crystalizes around you: the path you're on doesn't feel right. Perhaps the company's direction and yours have diverged, and you can now see that more clearly. Or the next step in your Possible Future is calling.

Once that initial tear in the fabric opens, it grows. The daily work doesn't energize you. When you're at work, you feel like a different person. Or maybe the tear happens suddenly, during a separation, or the company's sunsetting operations.

This chapter attempts to answer the question of "I sense I'm done here—what now?" We'll investigate the clues coming from this moment of discord, and detect what has shifted in your priorities. You may decide to step toward another organization, or to do something different entirely.

YOUR INFLECTION POINT

These events come about when something breaks your values, your honor, or your ego in such a strong way that you have what the Conscious Leadership Group calls a "whole body 'no'" reaction (https://bkaprt.com/scw48/08-01). You want *out*. Your head, heart, and gut are giving you a strong signal that this isn't the place for you.

Inside that strong reaction is a glimmer of what you want *instead*. It can take a while to tease out that information. Investigate the sensation. As we dig into a few themes I've seen, ask yourself if any of them match what you're feeling.

Not aligned with the next stage

For some folks, the tensions that come up as the company expands inhibit their ability to do their best work. Losing autonomy in your tool choice, no longer seeing transparency in decision-making, or drifting from the mission are all common frustrations for early employees. These are all signs of scale—every company that reaches a certain size must optimize for the many, for consistency, by using systems and structure.

When you can't align with the company's next step, spend some time thinking about why. It's possible that you want something different or that you've grown in an area that you want to follow more.

You must have your "must-haves"

The moment I knew I had to leave is still so vivid. I had dozens of Microsoft Teams messages urgently pinging me to add lines of text to a jam-packed PowerPoint deck. The deck was 144 slides long and had no meaning to me. I didn't want to become the person I would *need* to be for the team to reach the next level. The business needed someone who enjoyed the work and thrived doing it.

The business planning activities required of an executive took me far away from the mission that originally motivated me. I liked being on the road, at schools, helping students and teachers. Or building features that would make their lives easier. I tried to get more involved in volunteer work: I joined a board, and a fund that invested in local businesses. But it became clear that mission-driven work is my magnet, and I had to follow that pull.

Following your Possible Future

For others, that moment is the realization that they won't grow past a certain point in the company. They've been passed over for promotion more than once, or leadership has made it clear they're looking for people with different backgrounds.

For Dana Lawson, it was about speed and progression. She told me that she looked around and realized:

> *I couldn't advance as quickly as I wanted to, and at my next startup I could make that big leap to a VP title. It's super important for folks from underrepresented groups to reach, and to see someone like me, a queer person, reach the top roles. That's really motivating for me, to forge a path for others to come next.*

Anyone will tell you that promotions are hard: you burn capital lobbying, they take time, and the increments in compensation aren't as high as they would be if you simply changed companies. And the larger the company, the more entrenched gatekeeping around promotion. Lawson clearly needed to move toward opportunities with fast growth potential.

Now, let's revisit your Possible Future to see if any of your criteria have shifted.

PRIORITIES FOR YOUR NEXT ROLE

As the company changes, it also changes you. You've evolved with it. You've adapted. It has stretched your awareness and point of view. Things have shifted, and the career must-haves you identified back in Chapter 2 may have changed, too.

Spend some time thinking about what has shifted in you:

- Have your criteria changed?
- Is their importance to you, or "weight," different now?

- Have you learned things from your current role that you want to take forward?

If you used the *Career Planning, without the Pain* workbook, great (https://bkaprt.com/scw48/08-02). Let's consider your must-haves in a new light. Go ahead and add any new criteria that you've learned are important to you, and their weight, as you see them today. If your those things have changed, that will also alter your Career Composite—perhaps significantly.

You might even try the entire loop all over again, to gain further insight on what has shifted in you. I know that my "inspirational people" have changed significantly over the past ten years. I used to admire people who were financially independent, doing business on their own terms. Later I'd evolve to admire folks who adhered to their values. Now I find myself drawn to thoughtfulness and to leaders with self-awareness. You've heard from a number of them in this book; if you ever get a chance to work with those folks, jump at it.

Once you've found what you want, it's time to resign. And because resignations can be such a fraught experience, let me share a method with you that's authentic and maintains relationships.

STEPPING BACK WITH GRACE

Resigning isn't exactly enjoyable, but having been on both sides of the conversation, there are few tactics that can make it go more smoothly. I call this the "resigning with grace" method:

- Use your "Possible Future" as a script to frame the decision about your growth.
- Understand that tension isn't necessarily bad.
- Find a successor, or recommend candidates (if it's appropriate).

Since this is a delicate conversation, and one that people don't tend to discuss candidly, I'm going to pull the curtain back and talk about the mechanics of resigning. Your decision tree here starts with what your relationship with your manager is like.

If your relationship with your manager is good...

Try to resign during your one-on-one or scheduled meeting, and reference your Possible Future directly. This is one of the *many* reasons that being frank with your manager about where you want to go with your career pays off. Good leaders respect employees who have ambitions and go after them. It can help you leave on a high note, as Erica Brescia recalled during our conversation:

> *One of my favorite employees had this sort of conversation: "I am delivering, but I am thinking in about a year or so I am going to leave." That is a dream scenario. If anything, we respect a person more, not less.*

In a similar vein, Graham Neray told me about his departure from MongoDB to start his own thing:

> *I knew that I wanted to start a company, so I had an open conversation with the CEO. I told them, "I will do whatever you need me to do in this job. You can have my life (more or less) for the next two or three years. But I'm going to start a company after that." And so when the time came we put in place a three-month sort of exit ramp, and then I left.*

While my direct reports may have groaned when I asked them to work on their Possible Futures, almost all of them are now working in the roles we identified together. When they resigned, I was in full support of their next step, and we were able to build on that relationship. I was later invited to one's wedding—*after* she left—and I just wrote a graduate school recommendation for another.

If your manager is one of the reasons you're leaving...

If you didn't feel safe sharing your Possible Future with your manager, I'm sorry. And I hope you find a better manager in your next role, or that you can be the manager others need. To move on from a difficult position, use your Possible Futures as the script to anchor the conversation if you're doing it via a one-on-one.

It helps to write out a literal script that you can turn to if tempers flare. You're following your goals; your career is your own business (literally) and no one else's. But don't use this opportunity to be smug or to teach them a lesson. This relationship isn't working, and you're not going to fix it now.

If the relationship is beyond repair, resigning via email and copying HR is always an option. However, this choice is a hard deletion. It will surprise your manager, perhaps during a squeeze when resources are tight.

In my opinion, managers need to have these conversations in order to get better as managers. But not everyone is interested in that goal (and also, that's not your job). Use the hard delete only if you feel you must.

If tempers flare...

Breakups are hard. You're essentially rejecting the organization, and managers can take that personally. When I resigned from a role early in my career, my boss got so livid that he took my badge immediately and had me escorted from the building. Yikes.

Fifteen years later we laugh about it, but in that moment his anger flared because he was hurt. He recently told me something quite sweet: "I knew you were going to take over the world, I just thought you were going to do it working for me."

Let me tell you, it did not feel great at the time.

That said, if it's a tense conversation, or an emotional one, it's actually a *good* sign. The organization needed you, or you were reliable, or you are irreplaceable. So even if your manager takes it personally, know that it's usually for one of those reasons, and that it's not on you. If they blame you or try to guilt you on your way out, that's only an additional signal that you've made the right choice.

TRANSITIONS

Lots of people are reevaluating where they want their lives to go entirely, surprising not just their managers, but also themselves. I write this in year three of the Covid pandemic, as the fumes of the Great Resignation have cleared, and we edge toward a recession. Many of us are questioning our priorities—about 33 percent of Americans under forty, in fact (https://bkaprt.com/scw48/08-03, subscription required).

If that includes you, you aren't necessarily stepping back to align with another organization. You're in transition.

Scholars who study the life course point to transitions as times of heightened reflection, confusion, and distress as people search for meaning (https://bkaprt.com/scw48/08-04). You aren't simply changing from one *job* to another; you're in the process of changing from one *person* to another.

And that brings about this thrashy period that scholar William Bridges calls "the Neutral Zone."

> *All transitions are composed of (1) an ending, (2) a neutral zone, and (3) a new beginning.*
> *People go through an in-between time when the old is gone but the new isn't fully operational. It is when the critical psychological realignments and repatternings take place. (https://bkaprt.com/scw48/08-05)*

The Neutral Zone is a slow kind of chaos. It can feel like life's cards have been thrown up in the air and they froze there—you keep waiting for them to land, neatly shuffled, ready for the next hand. But what's on the other side is totally unclear. All you know for sure is that what you *were* doing? That no longer fits.

Growth feels great, doesn't it? Just kidding—it's some of the hardest work of being a human, a.k.a. "identity development." We're seeing ourselves differently; we need to integrate that new notion of self .

Just ask new parents: they will tell you they no longer sweat the small stuff. For them, getting dressed in a whole full-on professional outfit, and out the door is a win, and that loud noises no longer bother them as much. They can cope; they have those muscles now.

The difficult part, in my experience, is having faith that there will be a new beginning on the other side of "The Neutral Zone." It's knowing that this time we're spending feels unproductive, and that our current struggle is worth it.

False starts and outdated measurements

Everywhere around me I see folks fighting to end the vacuum of the Neutral Zone: they send out a hundred résumés in a panicked job search, they sketch out five business plans they'll never use, they start a new job but quit after thirty days. And I'm not immune, either. I signed up for horticulture school, only to find it meant sitting in a classroom staring at PowerPoint slides.

Transitions can feel endless and foggy, and for those of us who are achievement-oriented, these false starts can feel like failure. While we're making different choices—*new* choices—it's hard to not to measure ourselves against an older rubric. That can come up as jealousy of folks who seem to have it "figured out," or strong feelings of ambivalence that pull you back into old patterns.

It's entirely possible that you need a new rubric.

Taking time

Dozens of former colleagues find themselves wanting a different kind of success, and it's taking them some time to define that. Natalie Nagele, the former CEO of Wildbit, recently sold the company and found herself in this transition space. She offered me a grounding thought exercise on this matter: how many "tens" do you have?

There's this idea that you live life in ten-year increments. I heard this from a fellow founder, who said to me, "Businesses take about ten years." So it's a good question to ask, how many more "tens" do you have? How many more adventures do you have in front of you? I don't think there are that many, so I want to make sure that the next one we pick is really meaningful. And that requires time.

Of the problems we could possibly dedicate our skills to, on a ten-year horizon, which of them really matter? Ten years puts us in a very different space than our puppy-brain startup culture usually asks of us. Here are some other thought experiments I've found useful during phases of transition:

- Can you afford to take a sabbatical or time off between positions?
- Which projects or people have you always wanted to collaborate with?
- How can I make investments today (with time, effort, work) that will compound tomorrow?

Doing this thinking is not inertia. Neither is taking time in your current role to ask these questions.

REVISED DEFINITIONS OF SUCCESS

One of my favorite questions Lara Hogan asks is, "What are you optimizing for?" It's a way of surfacing someone else's thought process and understanding their priorities. I wonder if we, as individuals in the tech industry, are questioning what we're optimizing for in our lives. We could be shifting away from primarily valuing extrinsic motivators like status, titles, and compensation.

I see others feeling pulled toward meaningful relationships and contributing to society. Those sorts of intrinsic motivators get correlated with eventual outcomes like well-being, happiness, and life satisfaction (https://bkaprt.com/scw48/08-06).

Coming out of the era of "quiet quitting" into a recession and an era of layoffs may force us to redefine what success looks like. Two tools I've found helpful in this area are thinking through what "enough" might look like, and what in your life you want *more* of.

Defining "enough"

Organizational design consultant Kara Lindstrom recently introduced me to this notion of *lagom*, which is the Swedish word for "just enough." I love this concept because it gets at "enough" from the lens of moderation: what is *just the right amount* needed, and no more? If we apply the notion of *lagom* to money, status, or other kinds of work success, we might free ourselves up to take on higher rungs in Maslow's Hierarchy of Needs.

When considering definitions of "enough," I find the writings of Lynne Twist to possess morsels of wisdom. According to Twist, the first "toxic myth" that we have around money is this notion that there is not enough. She unpacks some of our worst "hoarding" tendencies as a culture.

> *When we believe there is not enough, that resources are scarce, then we accept that some will have what they need and some will not. We rationalize that someone is destined to end up with the short end of the stick. (https://bkaprt.com/scw48/08-07)*

Twist asks us to think about "enough" on a global scale: if we let go of hoarding tendencies, that would free up resources to move to where they are needed.

Defining "more"

With your revised definition of "enough" on one side, ask yourself: "What do I want more of?" I find myself inspired by Seer Interactive CEO Wil Reynolds, who has defined what enough means for him and chronicles what that feels like in his series "Living a Life of Enough":

I want a different kind of "more."

My company could do more, I want to grow more, we could do more for our team, more for our clients, more for our industry and more for our community. So I'm hungry for MORE but not for me and it's time to eat. (https://bkaprt.com/scw48/08-08)

For me, this concept is a compelling decision-making tool. Even if the path far in the future feels foggy, asking yourself, "What do I want more of?" can be a small but meaningful step in the right direction.

PARTING WORDS

❝ *Everything that you are needing, someone else is needing, too. Everything you are healing for yourself you are healing for someone else, too.*
—JENNIFER ARMBRUST, ENTREPRENEUR (https://sister.is/proposals-for-the-feminine-economy)

Moving on, at its core, is about finding alignment with *yourself*: new challenges have presented themselves, and you're making changes to address them. From there, the cycle begins anew: you start your next role, and discover what you want out of that role or that relationship.

And as you transition from one role to find rhythm in another, make space to tell your story. What have you learned, and how has it changed you? Work has transformed who you are, and other people will only benefit from the knowledge of how you got there. As you begin to draw a line through your experiences, you'll see patterns in your own behavior you didn't notice before. You can also prevent frustration and confusion in others, who might wrestle with similar challenges. This is an appeal to offer your path as a template for others. The stories we hear in the world of work are too male and too white. *Fortune* reported that in the year 2020, as many bestselling business books were written by men named "John" as by women (https://bkaprt.com/scw48/08-09).

What if, instead of narratives about conquering the Fortune 500 or amassing power, we thought about business stories through the lens of growth and transformation? If work has significantly changed you, there is a strong chance your story of growth can help someone else. Perhaps if we view our stories as interrelated, as building a web of support, we can encourage more voices to come to the fore.

Katherine May, who wrote a book about tough transitions called *Wintering*, sees all of our transformation stories in relationship to one another:

> *Transformation is the business of winter. [...] You'll find wisdom in your winter, and once it's over, it's your responsibility to pass it on. And in return, it's our responsibility to listen to those who have wintered before us. It's an exchange of gifts in which no one loses out. (https://bkaprt.com/scw48/08-10)*

I wanted to write the book that I needed at frustrating inflection points in my career. But it's also an offering to the discipline at large. I'd love to see your story next.

ACKNOWLEDGMENTS

I'M FORTUNATE TO HAVE BEEN supported by excellent managers: the patient Michael Boezi, the firecracker Dickson Musslewhite, the understanding Pam Hersperger, the direct J. Philipp Schmidt, the curious Dr. Karen Brennan, the erudite Dr. Jessica Collier, and the sage Shanku Niyogi. Thank you for your wisdom. I admire you.

Thank you to many folks who took part in this book, among them Neha Batra, Ida Benedetto, Erica Brescia, Casey Greene, Dana Lawson, Chris McDermott, Mary Moore-Simmons, Graham Neray, Natalie Nagele, Rick Nucci, Deva Santiago, Tilde Ann Thurium, Lynn Wallenstein, and Cassidy Williams.

My utter appreciation to the reviewers who illuminated my blind spots and lent their expertise and support: Sass Allard, Arielle Brousse, Lara Hogan, Alex Hillman, Magdalena Lipinska, Kris Nisula, Ricky Robinett, Jen Sellers, Rob Spectre, Mike Swift, and Sara Wachter-Boettcher.

To all Educats, past and present—Divya, Mo, Scott, John, Joe, Lieke, Arelia, Nathaniel, Katie, Elena, Eric, Jen, Dhiraj, Elise and Juan Pa—I appreciate you. Many thanks to the excellent editorial posse at A Book Apart for holding this book to the highest standards: Katel LeDû, Lisa Maria Marquis, Jen Mediano, and Caren Litherland. Also, gracious thanks to the GitHub leadership team.

RESOURCES

Proposals for the Feminine Economy by Jennifer Armbrust (https://bkaprt.com/scw48/09-01).

Welcoming the Unwelcome and *When Things Fall Apart* by Pema Chodron (https://bkaprt.com/scw48/09-02).

The 15 Commitments of Conscious Leadership from Conscious Leadership Group, (https://bkaprt.com/scw48/09-03). If there is one book I wish all managers would read, this is it.

Composing a Life by Mary Catherine Bateson (https://bkaprt.com/scw48/09-04).

Help! I Have a manager! by Julia Evans (https://bkaprt.com/scw48/09-05). If you aren't getting what you want from your manager or leader, this book will give you a framework for understanding why—and what to do about it.

Getting to Yes: Negotiating Agreement without Giving In by Robert Fisher and William Ury (https://bkaprt.com/scw48/09-06). Does the word "negotiation" make you nervous? It won't after you read this.

Accelerate: Building and Scaling High Performing Technology Organizations by Nicole Forsgren, Jez Humble, and Gene Kim (https://bkaprt.com/scw48/05-06/).

Good Work: Where Excellence and Ethics Meet by Howard Gardner (https://bkaprt.com/scw48/09-07).

Resilient Management by Lara Hogan (https://bkaprt.com/scw48/09-08). I use Hogan's feedback framework constantly. It's brief, and every page has gems. She also covers Paloma Medina's material on identifying core needs using the BICEPS model (https://bkaprt.com/scw48/09-09).

Amy Hoy, "Is Bad Copy Killing Your Product?"(https://bkaprt.com/scw48/09-10). Hoy uses the "Pain, Dream, Fix" framework for copywriting, and her writing style is infectious.

Leadership Tarot by Kara Lindstrom (https://bkaprt.com/scw48/09-11).

Scaling People by Claire Hughes Johnson (https://bkaprt.com/scw48/09-12).

The Culture Map: Breaking through the Invisible Boundaries of Global Business by Erin Meyer (https://bkaprt.com/scw48/09-13). Meyer will help you understand how your message might be perceived across cultures.

Beyond the Resume by Pam Selle (https://bkaprt.com/scw48/09-14).

Badass: Making Users Awesome by Kathy Sierra (https://bkaprt.com/scw48/03-04). Sierra is the original badass and a marketing, writing, teaching, everything genius.

Krista Tippett's On Being podcast (https://bkaprt.com/scw48/09-15).

REFERENCES

Shortened URLs are numbered sequentially; the related long URLs are listed below for reference.

Chapter 1

01-01 https://www.penguinrandomhouse.com/books/547991/the-four-by-scott-galloway/

01-02 https://www.sciencedirect.com/science/article/abs/pii/004724849290081J?via%3Dihub

Chapter 2

02-01 https://www.mckinsey.com/featured-insights/leadership/changing-change-management

02-02 https://www.gsb.stanford.edu/exec-ed/programs/stanford-lead/curriculum/courses/decision-making

02-03 https://ijbed.org/cdn/issue_file/content_64612_18-02-20-10-17-36.pdf

Chapter 3

03-01 https://web.media.mit.edu/~mres/papers/kindergarten-learning-approach.pdf

03-02 https://brainrules.net/brain-rules/

03-03 https://stackingthebricks.com/how-i-increased-conversion-2-4x-with-better-copywriting/

03-04 https://www.oreilly.com/library/view/badass-making-users/9781491919057/

Chapter 4

04-01 https://www.tarabrach.com/blog-working-with-fear-article-in-modern-maturity-magazine/

04-02 https://hbr.org/2018/02/research-what-happens-to-a-startup-when-venture-capitalists-replace-the-founder, subscription required

04-03 https://www.davidcbaker.com/is-now-a-good-time-to-rip-that-band-aid-off

04-04 https://www.youtube.com/watch?v=F_aM6CVMefw

04-05 https://heathbrothers.com/books/switch/

04-06 https://hbr.org/2007/05/surviving-your-new-ceo, subscription required

04-07 https://pamselle.gumroad.com/l/beyondtheresume

04-08 https://thewebivore.com/burn-resume-finding-next-job-engineer/

04-09 https://pemachodronfoundation.org/product/when-things-fall-apart-book/

04-10 https://hbr.org/2009/03/after-layoffs-help-survivors

04-11 http://www.dfcoaching.com/articles/ARTICLE-The%20Human%20Aspects%20of%20Managing%20Change.pdf

04-12 https://www.tenpercent.com/podcast-episode/dolly-chugh-568

04-13 https://www.oreilly.com/library/view/rituals-for-work/9781119530787/

04-14 https://www.shambhala.com/welcoming-the-unwelcome-9781611805659.html

Chapter 5

05-01 https://anthrosource.onlinelibrary.wiley.com/doi/10.1525/aa.1956.58.3.02a00080

05-02 https://www.bcg.com/publications/2016/breaking-the-culture-barrier-in-postmerger-integrations

05-03 https://www.lennyspodcast.com/lessons-from-scaling-stripe/

05-04 https://www.nytimes.com/2021/10/22/technology/facebook-election-misinformation.html

05-05 https://www.gsb.stanford.edu/faculty-research/case-studies/google-china

05-06 https://www.joelonsoftware.com/2000/08/09/the-joel-test-12-steps-to-better-code/

05-07 https://www.oreilly.com/library/view/accelerate/9781457191435/

Chapter 6

06-01 https://finance.yahoo.com/quote/ABNB/financials?p=ABNB

06-02 https://www.levels.fyi/blog/what-are-career-levels-ladders.html

06-03 https://www.zippia.com/microsoft-careers-7480/

06-04 https://www.academia.edu/8162909/The_impact_of_organizational_culture_on_the_job_satisfaction_of_knowledge_worker

06-05 https://www.norulesrules.com/

06-06 https://hbr.org/2017/10/hiring-discrimination-against-black-americans-hasnt-declined-in-25-years, subscription required

Chapter 7

07-01 https://hbr.org/2016/11/getting-reorgs-right

07-02 https://docs.gitlab.com/ee/user/analytics/dora_metrics.html

07-03   https://www.bcg.com/publications/2016/breaking-the-culture-barri-
        er-in-postmerger-integrations

Chapter 8

08-01   https://conscious.is/concepts/leading-and-living-from-your-
        whole-body-yes

08-02   https://www.fortuna.ink/tools

08-03   https://www.washingtonpost.com/business/2021/08/16/us-workers-want-
        career-change

08-04   https://www.researchgate.net/publication/8602869_Personal_Growth_
        in_Adults%27_Stories_of_Life_Transitions

08-05   https://wmbridges.com/about/what-is-transition

08-06   https://journals.sagepub.com/doi/10.1177/0146167296223006

08-07   https://soulofmoney.org/

08-08   https://wilreynolds.medium.com/day-1-living-a-life-of-enough-part-i-
        832bbbc96e19

08-09   https://fortune.com/2020/12/20/women-bestselling-busi-
        ness-books-2020/, subscription required

08-10   https://katherine-may.co.uk/winterin

Resources

09-01   https://sister.is/proposals-for-the-feminine-economy

09-02   https://pemachodronfoundation.org/

09-03   https://conscious.is/15-commitments

09-04   https://groveatlantic.com/book/composing-a-life/

09-05   https://wizardzines.com/zines/manager/

09-06   https://www.williamury.com/books/getting-to-yes/

09-07   https://www.hachettebookgroup.com/titles/howard-e-gardner/good-wor
        k/9780465026081/?lens=basic-books

09-08   https://resilient-management.com/

09-09   https://www.palomamedina.com/biceps

09-10   https://stackingthebricks.com/is-bad-copy-killing-your-product/

09-11   https://leadershiptarot.com/

09-12   https://press.stripe.com/scaling-people

09-13   https://erinmeyer.com/books/the-culture-map/

09-15   https://onbeing.org/

INDEX

ABOUT A BOOK APART

We cover the emerging and essential topics in web design and development with style, clarity, and above all, brevity—because working designer-developers can't afford to waste time.

COLOPHON

The text is set in FF Yoga and its companion, FF Yoga Sans, both by Xavier Dupré. Headlines and cover are set in Titling Gothic by David Berlow.

 This book was printed in the United States using FSC certified papers.

ABOUT THE AUTHOR

 **Vanessa Gennarelli** is the principal of Fortuna, a change management firm, and the chief operating officer for Raise.dev. She has led cross-functional teams at rapidly growing organizations, including GitHub Education through its acquisition by Microsoft. While at one of the largest tech companies on the planet, she learned how to navigate cultural differences, integrate new processes, and help direct reports thrive through change.

With a background in instructional design, Vanessa has a master's degree in technology, innovation, and education (Harvard). She is a former research intern at MIT Media Lab and a graduate of the LEAD Program (Stanford Business School). At home in Philadelphia, she invests in small businesses through the Circle of Aunts and Uncles, a group dedicated to supporting local entrepreneurs. She also serves on the Board of Directors for the Circadium School of Contemporary Circus.

Printed in the USA
CPSIA information can be obtained
at www.ICGtesting.com
JSHW040542060923
47526JS00010B/17